— from the —
GARDEN
— to the —
KINGDOM

from the
GARDEN
to the
KINGDOM

God's Eternal Purpose, Plan and Provision

Rod Connell

TATE PUBLISHING
AND ENTERPRISES, LLC

From the Garden to the Kingdom
Copyright © 2011 by Rod Connell. All rights reserved.

No part of this publication may be reproduced, stored in a retrieval system or transmitted in any way by any means, electronic, mechanical, photocopy, recording or otherwise without the prior permission of the author except as provided by USA copyright law.

Scripture taken from the *New King James Version*®. Copyright © 1982 by Thomas Nelson, Inc. Used by permission. All rights reserved.

This book is designed to provide accurate and authoritative information with regard to the subject matter covered. This information is given with the understanding that neither the author nor Tate Publishing, LLC is engaged in rendering legal, professional advice. Since the details of your situation are fact dependent, you should additionally seek the services of a competent professional.

The opinions expressed by the author are not necessarily those of Tate Publishing, LLC.

Published by Tate Publishing & Enterprises, LLC
127 E. Trade Center Terrace | Mustang, Oklahoma 73064 USA
1.888.361.9473 | www.tatepublishing.com

Tate Publishing is committed to excellence in the publishing industry. The company reflects the philosophy established by the founders, based on Psalm 68:11,
"*The Lord gave the word and great was the company of those who published it.*"

Book design copyright © 2011 by Tate Publishing, LLC. All rights reserved.
Cover design by Shawn Collins
Interior design by Christina Hicks

Published in the United States of America
ISBN: 978-1-61346-822-7
Religion / Christian Life / General
12.05.10

ACKNOWLEDGMENTS

I would like to thank Kevin McCarthy and Jennifer Grassle for their generous help in preparing my manuscript in its formatted form. I do most of my writing with a yellow pad and pencil, so thanks, guys, for helping me to finally enter the twenty-first century! All your assistance is greatly appreciated.

DEDICATION

This book is dedicated to those overcomers throughout the ages who have faithfully followed the footprints of the Master and have left their own tracks for us to follow. And to my beloved wife and helpmate, Jane, who has been beside me every step of the way on our spiritual journey together.

Table of Contents

The Simple Truth 12
INTRODUCTION 13

PART ONE:
GOD'S ETERNAL PURPOSE 15

THE BIG PICTURE 17
THE MAKEUP OF MAN 21
A BRIEF HISTORY OF FALLEN MAN 25
    The Great Flood and Beyond 27
    The Rebellion at Babel 29
    The Call of Abraham 33
    Jacob 35
    The Story of Joseph 38
    Moses and the Coming of the Law 39

PART TWO:
GOD'S ETERNAL PLAN:
THE COMING OF CHRIST 45

THE GENEALOGY OF JESUS 49
    Matthew 1:1–17 49
THE BIRTH OF JESUS 53
THE GOSPEL OF THE KINGDOM 55
JOHN THE BAPTIST 57
TRUE REPENTANCE 61
THE BAPTISM OF JESUS 63
THE WILDERNESS TESTING 65
THE MINISTRY OF CHRIST BEGINS 71
THE SERMON ON THE MOUNT 73
    Those Who Mourn 77
    The Meek 78
    Spiritual Hunger and Thirst 79

    The Merciful... 81
    The Pure in Heart 83
    The Peacemakers.. 84
    The Blessings of Persecution.................................. 85
BEFORE GOING ON.. 87
THREE VIEWS OF THE KINGDOM OF HEAVEN ..91
THE FRUIT OF THE BEATITUDES........................... 95
A HIGHER LAW 99
THE LORD'S PRAYER 103
FURTHER TEACHINGS 109
THE PURPOSE OF THE PARABLES....................... 111
    The Parable of the Sower 112
    The Parable of the Tares 114
    The Parable of the Mustard Seed........................ 116
    The Parable of the Leaven 119
    The Parable of the Hidden Treasure 120
    The Parable of the Pearl 121
    The Parable of the Dragnet.................................. 123
PARABLES OF WATCHFULNESS 127
    The Parable of the Fig Tree 127
    As in the Days of Noah 130
    The Parable of the Master of the House 132
    The Parable of the Two Servants 134
    The Parable of the Ten Virgins 136
    The Parable of the Talents 139
    The Parable of the Sheep and the Goats 142
END-TIMES: THE JEWS... 147
RAPTURE.. 153
    One Picture of Rapture 158

PART 3:
THE ETERNAL PROVISIONS IN CHRIST................ 159

CRUCIFIED WITH CHRIST 161
CHRIST IN US.. 165
THE ETERNAL PURPOSE, RESTATED..................... 167
ESSENTIAL FOOD 171
ESSENTIAL FOOD II 175

COMMUNION	185
TWO WILDERNESSES	189
FOUNDATIONS	193
THREE CRUCIAL FACTS	199
POSITION TO EXPERIENCE	205
LOVE AND OBEDIENCE	209
FIRST LOVE	213
KINGDOM FRUIT	217
THE FULLNESS OF TIME	221
SUMMING UP	225
AFTERWORD	227
Kingdom Perspective	228
OTHER WORKS BY ROD CONNELL	229
Silly Snake Rhymes…And the Real Stuff	229
Songs of a Son	230

The Simple Truth

The gospel is Christ plus nothing,
No additives required;
Man's traditions complicating,
For by the flesh inspired…

Jesus Himself *is* the good news,
In *Him* is everything!
It is His *Person* that we choose;
He is His offering!

INTRODUCTION

For over thirty-five years, I have searched for God. Not unto salvation, for eternal Life is securely mine; and not for what man has made of Him, but for God Himself. Satan, after his defeat at the cross, has been driven to confound and weaken the Body of Christ. His survival, after all, has depended upon it. Spiritually, it has been one long chess game, which I believe is reaching its conclusion. The enemy is running out of moves.

Deception has been our foe's main weapon, to keep sinners lost in sin as well as to stunt the growth of believers; anything to prevent the full manifestation of the sons of God. Tares were planted amidst the wheat; false teaching crept in early on and has persisted from the days of Paul to the present. The beloved apostle, in fact, spent a great deal of his time not only planting new churches but keeping the existing ones free of the infiltration and distortions of Satan.

In the Sermon on the Mount, Jesus promised that those who hunger and thirst after righteousness shall be filled—not only in the future Millennium but now. I can testify to the truth of that promise: the Holy Spirit has filled me again and again, at times when my strength was almost gone. And in the process has revealed many hidden treasures, essential keys to the return of the Lord.

Three revelations stand out:

1. The eternal purpose of God.
2. The plan to achieve that purpose.
3. The provisions within the plan to ensure His purpose's success.

The eternal purpose of God is for His Son to be the sum of all things, that He would be all-in-all, meaning that everything in the Heavens and on the earth be filled with nothing but the Life and glory of Christ. Christ Himself, coming to earth as a man, born of woman and under the Law, *is* the plan to bring about that eternal purpose. His perfect life and sacrificial death on the cross set the plan into motion. But His first coming was for far more than dying for the sins of all who will come to Him in repentance and faith.

Within the plan, of course, there had to be provisions that would ensure the fulfillment of God's great purpose. Without those provisions—practical steps taken by faith in the revealed Word of God—neither the purpose nor the plan could come to fruition. It is *my* purpose to clearly spell out our provisions in Christ, to indeed see Satan's days on the earth come to an end and the coming of the Kingdom, the next stage in the fulfillment of God's eternal purpose.

Purpose, plan, and provision. With these three revelations, all the rest of Scripture and the history of mankind now make sense.

PART ONE: GOD'S ETERNAL PURPOSE

To me, who am less than the least of all the saints, this grace was given, that I should preach among the Gentiles the unsearchable riches of Christ, and make all see what is the fellowship of the mystery, which from the beginning of the ages has been hidden in God who created all things through Christ; to the intent that *now* the manifold wisdom of God might be made known by the church to the principalities and powers in the Heavenly places, according to *the eternal purpose* which He accomplished in Christ Jesus our Lord, in whom we have boldness and access with confidence through faith in Him.

Ephesians 3:8–12

He is the image of the invisible God, the firstborn over all creation. For by Him all things were created that are in Heaven and that are on earth, visible and invisible, whether thrones or dominions or principalities or powers. All things were created through Him and for Him. And he is before all things, and in Him all things consist. And He is the head of the body, the church, who is the beginning, the firstborn from the dead, that in all things He may have the preeminence.

Colossians 1:15–18

THE BIG PICTURE

Upon becoming new believers in the Lord Jesus Christ, we begin to make progress piecemeal, a little here, a little there. Secure that we have truly been saved from the judgment of this world and will someday enter Heaven, we begin our Christian walk as newborn babes, trying earnestly to make sense of the Word of God and to live a life pleasing to God. But in spite of the fact that the Holy Spirit has been sent to guide us into all truth, this task seems monumentally daunting, and the Bible an extraordinarily intricate and complex puzzle.

Little by little, we begin to understand certain essential truths while others just do not seem to fit. But we know that the Lord Himself promised that we will be blessed if we continue to hunger and thirst after righteousness. So if we press on, He keeps that promise, gives us new revelations and insights, and we progress in our walk.

And yet we find ourselves not quite grasping the whole. We yearn to be delivered from the power as well as the penalty of sin and to live a life of holiness unto the Lord. But if we are honest with ourselves, we come to realize that we are falling short; sin's power overtakes us at times, robbing us of the joy and the peace that should be ours. We make new resolutions to resist, redouble our efforts in prayer and Bible study, and for a time seem to be doing better. But soon we find ourselves, once again, in defeat.

The problem, of course, is that unknowingly we are pursuing God in our own power and going after *things*; good things to be sure, like sanctification, humility, patience, the fruit of the Spirit. In our pursuit of these things, of course, it is our well-intentioned purpose to try so hard to be like Jesus.

But eventually frustration and even despair set in, as we begin to see we simply cannot do it. Throwing ourselves on the grace and mercy of God, we have actually arrived at a very good place, the place where God has been waiting for us all along, waiting for us to reach the end of ourselves. For those who reach this point and have not given up, the Holy Spirit will show the way.

For me, this came in a most astounding way. The Lord showed me that it is not about me at all. I had been trying to make sense of all the pieces of the puzzle, but in my own power, always relating everything back to myself. It was as if the Holy Spirit suddenly showed me the box top of the puzzle, the picture showing the Father's eternal purpose, the reason for everything that ever existed, even myself—the master key that makes all the countless, individual pieces begin to fit, solving the mystery of time and eternity.

What is the eternal purpose of God that was conceived and ordained from before the foundations of the world? One thing, and one thing only: that His Son might be the sum of all things. Quite simply stated, but astounding in its scope, that Christ might be all-in-all, that everything in the universe, beginning with man, be filled with nothing but the Life and glory of Christ. In the light of that revelation, I could see that outside Christ, there is nothing of any spiritual value whatsoever, that He is our everything. Holiness does not exist outside Him; *He* is holiness. Righteousness does not exist outside Him, for He Himself is righteousness. And so it is with sanctification, patience, humility, meekness, and all other spiritual virtues and goals. Christ is to be everything!

Do you see what that means? We *cannot* be like Jesus; we cannot by certain efforts truly come to imitate Christ. All such attempts will prove futile. I had been trying so hard to change, to become holy and pleasing to God, to abstain from evil and to do good instead. But no matter how hard I tried or prayed, I always ended up failing. Once this new revelation began to sink in, I initially felt elated, relieved. I would not have to keep failing at something I could never achieve, nor feel such frustration and despair over my failures.

But then as time went on, I found myself in a very awkward condition. I knew that my old ways of pursuing God were worthless, but I did not know how to look for Him in the new light the Spirit had revealed. For some time, I was in a malaise, very passive, not trusting myself anymore, but not knowing how to go on to what the Lord had shown me.

The Spirit then led me to study more closely the fall of man and the rebellion of Satan, what God had originally intended when He created man, and how the enemy had thwarted that plan. Satan had rebelled long before man was created and had been cast down from the presence of God. His rebellion had caused a severe breach: the authority of God had been challenged for the first time. So far as we know, up until that time, God's rule was perfect and unobstructed. The holiness and sovereignty of God could not allow such an affront.

So in time, as His remedy, God created man—a creation made to defeat the enemy and return absolute rule to God. His plan was to fill man with both His Life and His glory, and thereby win the victory, becoming once again the God of Heaven *and* earth. To that end, Genesis tells us that He created man in His own image and likeness, letting man "have dominion over the fish of the sea, over the birds of the air, and over the cattle, over all the earth and over every creeping thing that creeps on the earth" (Genesis 1:26).

That dominion, power, and control given to man was to include Satan and his fallen host!

But of course, things did not work out that way. Satan found a way through deception to corrupt man and woman to follow his ways instead of God's. As a consequence, man was also banished from the presence of God and went about the earth being as god himself, doing what was right in his own eyes. Thus the long and tragic history of mankind, estranged from God, with seemingly no way back to his Maker.

Next, I began to look at man himself: what had happened to him when he chose himself over God? What in our makeup was altered that sad day in Eden? What needed to be recovered to reestablish our dominion over all creation and bring about God's eternal purpose? How in our fallen state could Christ ever become all-in-all in our lives?

THE MAKEUP OF MAN

Genesis 1:26 tells of God's plan for man: the Godhead decided to create man in a special way: first of all, he was not to be spoken into existence, as were other parts of creation, but handled and breathed into life by the Spirit of God; and he was to be made in the very image and likeness of God Himself. I take that to be a three-part being, body, soul, and spirit. Many believe that man is only a two-part creation, body and soul, that soul and spirit are one and the same. But that interpretation does not square with Hebrews 4, verse 12 or 1 Thessalonians 5:23:

> For the word of God is living and powerful, and sharper than any two-edge sword, piercing even to the division of soul and spirit, and of joints and marrow, and is a discerner of the thoughts and intents of the heart.
>
> Hebrews 4:12

And Paul blessed the believers at Thessalonica with these words:

> Now may the God of peace Himself sanctify you completely; and may your whole spirit, soul and body be preserved blameless at the coming of our Lord Jesus Christ.
>
> 1 Thessalonians 5:23

At the moment of the creation of man, the Scripture reads:

> And the Lord God formed man of the dust of the ground, and breathed into his nostrils the breath of life; and man became a living soul.
>
> Genesis 2:7

Dust and the breath of God combined to create a living being; the dust being the substance, or body, the breath of God the spirit, and the end product, a living creature with a soul. The soul of man is made up of his mind, his will, and his emotions, his very personality, his psuche (self). The body, of course, includes the physical portion, which is in contact with the outside world through man's five senses. The spirit of man is the realm wherewith the Spirit of God is able to communicate with man, for He is a Spirit and those who wish to worship, or commune, with Him must do so "in spirit" as well as in truth. So, as somebody has aptly put it, the body is for world-consciousness, the soul for self-consciousness, and the spirit for God-consciousness.

When Eve, then Adam, sinned, they were cast from the Garden, where they had enjoyed such direct Spirit-to-spirit intimacy with God. Their spirits became as though dead, direct communication with God cut off. The enemy had promised that they would become as god themselves, knowing good and evil, and in a twisted sort of way, that is exactly what happened. By declaring their independence from God, and by stepping out of their proper domain as man over into the realm of deity, they did in fact become their own gods. It was almost as if God said, "You want to be as Me yourself, go ahead. Let's see how that works out for you." And He let them go.

Of course, with the spirit essentially inoperative, the soul became the center of their existence. The soul (their own mind, will, and emotions) ascended to the throne, the place God had ordained to be filled by their spirits; it was now the soul that directed all of life's activities. They still bore a certain likeness to their Maker, but the inner image had been lost.

This is the condition, as children of Adam, in which we all enter life. And it was this condition that Jesus came to address, redeem, and heal. Being born again, after all, is the process by which the Holy Spirit is the agent of conception, convicting the old life of sin and separation from God, and then through true repentance and belief in Christ, breathing new Life into our spirits, restoring and enabling the spirit once again to commune with God.

By grace, through faith have we all who are believers been saved. Through belief in the shed blood of the Lord Jesus Christ as atonement for our sins, eternal life is ours; freely given, through no merit of our own. But once our spirits have new Life, another battle begins. Our souls have been command central for so long that they do not abdicate the throne automatically. And the spirit does not take the throne by force. We see that we have served evil and the enemy before coming to God. So we resolve that we will forsake that life and serve God and good instead.

This is exactly the path Satan wants us to take. For this is the path to defeat. The tree from which our ancient ancestors ate in the Garden was the tree of the knowledge of good as well as evil. So, to try by the strength of the flesh to "know" good is as fatal as following after evil. These are both the fruit of the same tree, the tree of death.

The "flesh" is far more than the physical or carnal parts of man. The flesh is anything with which we were born naturally— not only physical bodies, but also a certain degree of intelligence, emotions, and the ability to choose (the will). These too are part of the flesh. So to merely will, or decide, to follow the way of goodness and God instead of the way of Satan and sin is a fruitless enterprise. The Word declares that which is born of the flesh is flesh, and only that which is born of the Spirit is

Spirit. In other words, flesh can never give birth to spirit. And to simply will one way or the other is of the flesh, about which Paul declared: "In the flesh dwelleth no good thing" (Romans 7:18).

So what is the path to victory? How do we make Christ all-in-all in our lives, the sum of all things that we are? The Word declares through Paul, by the way, that the very center of God is none other than Christ Himself and that this was a great mystery throughout the ages. The revelation of this mystery was first revealed to Paul—the mystery of God, even Christ, hidden in the heart of God—who has now revealed it to us. And yet, it is almost as if the enemy was able to hide this essential truth all over again.

Men began to try to achieve holiness, to be humble, patient, longsuffering, as things, virtues outside the person of Christ Himself. But all such efforts are doomed to failure. For Christ is not only the sum of all things, but also all the addends as well, *all-in-all!* He alone is all that we strive and long for. So, as one saint has said so well, "we are not to have changed lives, but rather *exchanged* lives; our life exchanged for His" (Gal. 2:20).

In the words of Blaise Pascal:

> There is a God-shaped vacuum in the heart of every man, which cannot be filled by any created thing, but only by God, the Creator, made known through Jesus.
>
> Pascal, Blaise: *Pensées*

Once that void is filled with the Life and glory of Christ in all who are His, the creation of man will finally be complete; in the meanwhile, we are a work "in progress."

Before we discuss how the Father's great purpose is to be brought into manifestation, let us briefly explore the history of man's efforts on earth without the Life and glory of Christ at the core of his being. Indeed, mankind has accomplished many marvelous feats in his godless journey, but in spite of all his successes and "progress," peace has eluded him and alienation from God has persisted.

A BRIEF HISTORY OF FALLEN MAN

> And the Lord God said, 'Behold, the man is become as one of us, to know good and evil: and now, lest he put forth his hand, and take also of the tree of life, and eat and live forever'—therefore the Lord God sent him out of the garden of Eden to till the ground from which he was taken. So He drove out the man; and He placed cherubim at the east of the garden of Eden, and a flaming sword which turned every way, to guard the way of the tree of life.
>
> Genesis 3:22–23

In an impaired condition, the soul now ruling over the spirit (deviated by sin from God's original intention), man was driven from the Garden of Eden. By her act of spiritual adultery, Eve, followed by her husband, had unwittingly ensured that the law of sin and death would perpetuate itself throughout the generations of mankind. So to make certain that man did not eat of the tree of life in his fallen state, the Lord God thrust Adam and Eve from His presence, and posted cherubim and a flaming sword that turned in all directions to prevent access to the Garden and the tree. Serious sin followed almost immediately.

"And Cain talked with Abel his brother: and it came to pass, when they were in the field, that Cain rose up against Abel his brother, and slew him" (Genesis 4:8).

Cain, Adam and Eve's firstborn, was a tiller of the ground. Abel, his brother and the second-born son, was a shepherd. Each of them brought a sin-offering to the Lord. Cain brought the fruit of the ground which he had grown, and Abel brought of the firstborn of his flock and its fat to the Lord. God accepted Abel's offering, but rejected Cain's.

There have been many ideas as to the reason for His acceptance and rejection: both sons were then sinners, so they each needed to offer the Lord an offering for their sins. But the Scriptures tell us in another place that there is no remission of sins except through the shedding of blood. So on these grounds, Cain's offering was unacceptable. Others have suggested that Cain knew this, and yet simply wanted to do things in his own way, independent of the commands of the Lord. This is entirely possible, for such is the way of sinful man (his own fallible soul ruling over him instead of his spirit under the guidance of the Holy Spirit).

In any case, the Lord gave Cain an opportunity to repent. But his anger was so great that he rose up and killed his brother instead. In his eyes, Cain did not feel that his treatment by God was fair. So rather than submitting to the authority of the Lord, he took authority into his own hands and executed what *he* deemed to be justice.

For this transgression, God put a mark upon Cain and sent him farther away from His presence, to the land of Nod, east of Eden, and He cursed the ground that Cain would thenceforth till, restricting the earth's yield from his efforts, due to the blood of his brother which he had spilled in Eden. But the mark of God upon Cain was also a sign of God's mercy, even in the midst of judgment, for it protected Cain from being killed as he wandered about as a fugitive and a vagabond.

The tragic history of man, doing what is right in his own eyes rather than allowing his Maker to direct his actions, was then set into full motion. The first murder, the killing of another human, created in the image and likeness of God, brought on by anger, jealousy and hatred, defiled the land; a seed planted that would reproduce itself over and over again and proliferate into the bloody wars and massacres lying yet in the future.

The Great Flood and Beyond

> And God saw that the wickedness of man was great in the earth, and that every imagination of the thoughts of his heart was only evil continually. And it repented the Lord that He had made man on the earth, and it grieved Him at His heart. And the Lord said, 'I will destroy man whom I have created from the face of the earth'... but Noah found grace in the eyes of the Lord.
>
> Genesis 6:8

In only a few generations, it began to grieve the Lord that He had ever created mankind, and He purposed in His heart to wipe them from the face of the earth. The sin situation from the days of Cain and Abel had grown and grown to the point that even the thoughts, as well as the deeds of mankind, had become exceedingly and continually evil.

But as in all generations, God had a small remnant who found favor in His eyes, in this case only a single family. So, even as judgment was about to fall, grace and mercy were not forgotten. Noah's seed was to survive, thus ensuring that the human race would not be altogether blotted out, nor the eternal purpose of God eliminated.

After warning the righteous Noah and instructing him to build a great ark, the rain began to fall for forty days and forty nights, until the entire earth was under water. All life, except

Noah's family and the animals he had been commanded to save, was destroyed. When the waters finally receded, mankind was granted a new start, with a promise from God that the earth would never again be destroyed by water.

But of course, it was not long until the cycle of sin and death began to repeat itself. Noah planted a vineyard and became drunk from the wine that was produced from the fruit. While this was indeed a poor choice on the part of Noah, a far more serious sin was to arise in the heart of his son, Ham, who witnessed his father's transgression:

> And Noah began to be a farmer, and he planted a vineyard. Then he drank of the wine and was drunk, and became uncovered in his tent. And Ham, the father of Canaan, saw the nakedness of his father, and told his brothers outside. But Shem and Japheth took a garment, laid it on both shoulders, and went backward and covered the nakedness of their father. Their faces were turned away, and they did not see their father's nakedness.
>
> Genesis 9:20–23

There is a great lesson to learn from this story. In addition to man having rebelled against the direct authority of God, he then added to his sin by not respecting God's delegated authority. Noah was the head of his family, and God's delegated authority over the earth at that time.

Ham, rather than seeing the dignity of his father's authority and protecting it, was quick to find fault with it, exposing it for others to see. Such is the natural tendency of fallen man, to rebel against any authority that does not meet with his own approval, starting with the authority of God and extending to rebellion against God's delegated authorities.

Scripture informs us that no authority exists on earth that has not been delegated by God; therefore, rebellion against any authority, whether in the family, the church, or the government, is rebellion against God Himself. All sins, as separate acts of unrighteousness, flow from this one basic cause: rebellion. It began with Lucifer and by his influence has infected the sons of man. God, therefore, deals quite harshly with all such cases.

In the case of Ham, a curse was spoken by his father and has come to pass in the descendants of Ham. He and the offspring of his loins did indeed become slaves to the children of Shem and Japheth. In reading the genealogy of Ham, we find them to be among the ones in the promised land of Canaan that the children of Israel displaced during the times of Moses and Joshua, many of the various "-ites" who were to become the enemies of the children of God's promise... a most grave consequence of rebellion against authority

The Rebellion at Babel

> So God blessed Noah and his sons, and said to them: 'Be fruitful and multiply, and fill the earth.'
>
> Genesis 9:1

> And they said, 'Come, let us build ourselves a city, and a tower whose top is in the Heavens; let us make a name for ourselves, lest we be scattered abroad over the face of the earth.'
>
> Genesis 11:4

After the flood-waters receded, and God blessed Noah and his sons, setting a rainbow in the sky as a sign that He would never again destroy all flesh by water, the nations began to gradually emerge—the offspring of Ham, Shem, and Japheth. The Lord had commanded the survivors of the flood to multiply and fill the earth.

But the descendants of Ham decided to remain on the plains of Shinar and not spread themselves abroad as the Lord had commanded. Instead, they would build a city and a great tower reaching the Heavens, making a name for themselves. The leader of this endeavor was a man named Nimrod, son of Cush, the son of Ham. Nimrod was a mighty man, the Word proclaims, and indeed he founded his own kingdom, beginning at Babel and eventually extending into Assyria, including the city of Nineveh.

The project at Babel was the epitome of rebellion, man doing things according to his own will and by his own power. Babel, which means "confusion," was located in what is today known as Iraq. It is the root of the word "Babylon," the capital of Nebuchadnezzar's great Babylonian empire many centuries later. The Babylonian way of life had two main thrusts: the efforts of the flesh for self-glorification, and a system of false religion, man choosing his own gods.

King Nebuchadnezzar was harshly chastened by the Lord God for these same offenses. The king had a golden image created, immense in size (seventy-five feet high and nine feet wide!) and commanded that all those in his kingdom should bow down and worship the image when a symphony of music was heard. The penalty of refusal was death by being cast into a fiery furnace.

The three Israelites, Shadrach, Meshach, and Abednego, as we all know, refused to bow down and worship the golden image and indeed were thrown into the burning furnace. When God intervened and miraculously spared the lives of the faithful three, the king was so impressed, he promoted the Hebrew men to high posts in the kingdom.

At this point in time, it seemed that Nebuchadnezzar had changed; for Daniel, chapter 4 starts out with the king praising the one true God:

> To all peoples, nations, and languages that dwell in the earth: Peace be multiplied to you. I thought it good to declare the signs and wonders that the Most High God has worked for me. How great are His signs, and how mighty His wonders! His Kingdom is an everlasting kingdom, and His dominion is from generation to generation.
>
> Daniel 4:1–3

But this account was followed by the king's second dream, which Daniel interpreted. Nebuchadnezzar was warned in the dream to repent of his sins and great pride. Daniel even named the consequence if he did not repent. But for whatever reason, the king did not obey. So, twelve months later, as Nebuchadnezzar was walking about the palace, his heart once again swelled in pride, the king said,

> 'Is not this great Babylon, that I have built for a royal dwelling by my mighty power and for the honor of my majesty?' While the word was still in the king's mouth, a voice fell from Heaven: 'King Nebuchadnezzar, to you it is spoken: the kingdom has departed from you! And they shall drive you from men, and your dwelling shall be with the beasts of the field. They shall make you eat grass like oxen; and seven times shall pass over you, until you know that the Most High rules in the kingdom of men, and gives it to whomever He chooses.'
>
> Daniel 4:30–32

After the seven years of the prophecy were fulfilled, the king did indeed come to his senses, his kingdom was restored, and he forever after, I believe, worshiped the God of Heaven. But although the story of Nebuchadnezzar had a happy ending, the Babylonian doctrine and way of life did not. It continued and thrived, eventually spreading in one form or another to all nations. The final judgment of God will fall on this satanic creation, as stated in Revelation, chapter 18.

Some Biblical scholars believe that the Babylon spoken of in this chapter is an actual city, the center of trade and economics during the end-times. I personally think it is more likely to be speaking of the destruction of the Babylonian system and world-view. Either way, the judgment of the Lord will come upon Babylon even as it did upon King Nebuchadnezzar, but with no hope of mercy or repentance:

> And I heard another voice from Heaven saying, 'Come out of her, my people, lest you share in her sins, and lest you receive of her plagues. For her sins have reached to Heaven, and God has remembered her iniquities. Render to her just as she rendered to you, and repay her double according to her works; in the cup which she has mixed, mix double for her. In the measure that she glorified herself and lived luxuriously, the same measure give her torment and sorrow; for she says in her heart, 'I sit as a queen, and am no widow, and will not see sorrow.' Therefore her plagues will come in one day—death and mourning and famine. And she will be utterly burned with fire, for strong is the Lord God who judges her.'
>
> Revelation 18:4–8

Thus we can see a strong cord of rebellion running from the days of Nimrod and Babel to the establishment of a kingdom based on the same principles, to a world-wide infection: man living independently from the God of Heaven, creating glory unto himself and serving gods of his own making; his soul ruling over his spirit, which eventually leads to judgment and destruction.

At Babel, the Lord came down and confused the language of the people, which shut down the work on the city and tower, causing them to scatter abroad. But this was only a temporary solution, for they took their fallen nature with them wherever they went, allowing Satan to build and expand his kingdom throughout the earth as the prince of this world.

From all these tragic stories, it can be clearly seen that mankind had wandered far away from God's original intentions and purpose. (We too were in that condition before coming to Christ.) But God was about to call unto Himself a peculiar people, those He could begin to work through to eventually bring forth His eternal purpose of making Christ the sum of all things.

The Call of Abraham

> Now the Lord had said unto Abram, 'Get thee out of thy country, and from thy kindred, and from thy father's house, unto a land I will show thee: And I will make of thee a great nation, and I will bless, and make thy name great; and thou shalt be a blessing: and I will bless them that bless thee, and curse him that curseth thee: and in thee shall all the families of the earth be blessed.'
>
> Genesis 12:1–3

From the line of Shem, Noah's son, later to be called Semites, God appeared to Abram in the Ur of the Chaldees to call forth unto himself a people. Abram and his family were no different from the other inhabitants of that region; they were idolaters with no real knowledge of the one true God. And yet the Spirit of the Lord called Abram to leave his land and his father, his very life and past, to journey to a place the Lord would show him later.

And with the call came great and mighty promises: that he who had no children would become the father of a nation, that his very name would become great, that all the families of the earth would be blessed because of him. And that God Himself would protect him, blessing those who blessed Abram and cursing those who cursed him.

After initially faltering, not leaving as commanded until Terah, his father, died in Haran, and taking with him his nephew, Lot, and his family, Abram set out. God at last had his man, his called out one, one whom He could mold until he would become known as the father of the faith of those who believe God; from which in due time the "seed of the woman" prophesied in Genesis 3 would emerge. A turn toward the eternal purpose of God had finally been made.

The lessons of Abram were long and hard, and in his soulish condition (for nothing was indeed different in his makeup from any other man), he often failed. From fear for his own life, twice he lied, saying Sarai was not his wife but his sister. Growing impatient for the birth of his promised son, he listened to his wife and fathered a son by Hagar, Sarai's Egyptian handmaiden. This offspring of the flesh, Ishmael, due to the promised blessing on the seed of Abraham, also sired twelve tribes; but the descendants of Ishmael became and remain a thorn in the side of Israel to this very day.

But Abram, renamed Abraham before the birth of Isaac, learned well the lessons of faith, and *that* faith, as limited and imperfect as it was, became counted as righteousness unto him. (Romans 4:9). The supreme act of the faith of Abraham came when God called for the sacrifice of the very son of promise, who had finally come twenty-five years after the Lord had spoken it. Abraham was to bring Isaac to Mt. Moriah and there offer him as a sacrifice to the Lord.

What a test!

And yet Abraham quickly obeyed! We do not know for sure what must have gone through his mind. His faith in God had matured immensely over the years, and he must have known that God cannot lie. After all, Isaac was the promised seed through whom all the families of the earth were to be blessed. How could that happen were his son to die? Hebrews 11, the great faith chapter, puts it this way:

> By faith Abraham, when he was tested, offered up Isaac, and he who had received the promises offered up his only begotten son, of whom it was said, 'In Isaac your seed shall be called,' concluding that God was able to raise him up, even from the dead, from which he also received him in a figurative sense.
>
> Hebrews 11:17–19

Of course Isaac was spared, and he in turn fathered Jacob, who was the next heir of the great promises God had made to his grandfather, Abraham.

Jacob

Jacob is a perfect example of serving God from the soul and not the spirit, working hard to bring about the fulfillment of the promised blessings of God by human effort. So many true believers continue to work like Jacob, knowing the blessings that are theirs, but rather than waiting for God to deliver them in His own time, they strive and struggle to produce them themselves. Such a walk will only result in crisis after crisis, even as it did in the life of Jacob.

In Genesis 25, just before the birth of the twins Jacob and Esau, when their mother, Rebekah, inquired of the Lord as to the cause of all the turmoil in her womb as she carried the boys to term, the Lord said to her: "Two nations are in your womb, two peoples shall be separated from your body; one people shall be stronger than the other, and the older shall serve the younger" (Genesis 25:22–23). So the Lord's blessing was to be upon Jacob and not Esau; Rebekah had the word of the Lord on it.

As the boys grew, they were very different: Esau was a ruddy, hairy man who loved to hunt, a man of the field; in today's parlance, a "man's man." But Jacob was a mild man, staying close to hearth and home. The Word clearly indicates that Esau was

Isaac's favorite, but Jacob was the apple of his mother's eye. This favoritism by the parents played greatly into the brothers' futures.

In two crucial episodes, Jacob proved true to his name, for he was indeed, in the beginning, a schemer and a supplanter. Esau came in from the field one day and was weary and hungry. Jacob had cooked a lentil stew, and the famished Esau pleaded for some of it. Jacob agreed, but with this condition attached: "But Jacob said, 'Swear to me your birthright as of this day'" (Genesis 25:31). In the culture of that period, the father's blessing went to the firstborn, even a double portion. But Esau foolishly forfeited his birthright for the sake of a full stomach. And the last verse of Genesis 25 ends with these sad words: "Thus Esau despised his birthright" (Genesis 25:34).

Later, near the end of Isaac's life, Jacob was guilty of an even more despicable act. At the suggestion of his mother, Jacob fooled his nearly blind father into thinking he, Jacob, was indeed Esau. It was time for the aged father to bless his firstborn, so he called for Esau to bring him some stew made from the game his son had killed, that he might bless him before he died. Of course most of us know the rest of the story: Jacob and his mother went to great lengths to fool Isaac, so that Jacob, and not Esau, might receive the blessing; which is exactly what happened, and once the blessing was given, it could not be taken back.

Esau returned home from hunting only to find that his brother had received the blessing which should have been the firstborn's. There being no remedy for the situation, Esau was filled with hatred for his brother. He even vowed to kill him for his treachery: "So Esau hated Jacob because of the blessing with which his father blessed him, and Esau said in his heart: 'The days of mourning for father are at hand; then I will kill my brother Jacob'" (Genesis 27:41).

This was the first of many crises in the life of Jacob, each as a result of his own scheming ways to bring about the blessings of God which were actually already his. We will explore the purpose of such crises in a later chapter, but for now we will confine ourselves to the topic at hand.

The Lord allowed Jacob to pass from crisis to crisis, and strangely enough, never once reprimanded him openly for his errant ways. And neither did He ever annul His promises. It took one last crisis for Jacob to finally get the point. The Lord spoke to Jacob, telling him to return home to face his brother, Esau; and furthermore God promised Jacob that things would go well for Jacob for his obedience.

But for this occasion, Jacob had yet another scheme: to win his brother's favor, he would send his wives and children before him, with many livestock as a gift to Esau. Surely his brother would see these tokens of appeasement and relent of his hatred. He would also divide his family, servants, and possessions into two groups, so that should Esau attack, at least one group might escape.

Alone at night, as he waited for morning, when he himself would cross the river into Seir, a man appeared and wrestled with Jacob until the breaking of day. The man, seeing he could not prevail against Jacob, touched the socket of his hip, dislocating it. Jacob would forever limp and have to lean upon a staff for the rest of his life.

But his wound was actually a blessing: I believe it taught Jacob to never again lean upon his own strength and understanding, but upon God alone ... the mark of God, a painful reminder of the old Jacob. And indeed even his name was changed that day. The man (the pre-incarnate Christ?) would not tell Jacob his own name, but he did change Jacob's:

> So He said to him, 'What is your name?' He said, 'Jacob.' And He said, 'Your name shall no longer be called Jacob, but Israel; for you have struggled with God and with men, and have prevailed,' ... And He blessed him there.
>
> Genesis 32:27–29

Not only was his name changed that day, but Jacob himself was changed: no more the schemer and conniver, but a man who would truly rest in the blessings of God. Of all the men in the Old Testament, none ended up any better than Jacob; nay, Israel! (And his brother, Esau, by the way, met him with tears and open arms when they were reunited; surely the Lord had gone before him, even as He had promised. The Lord is always faithful!)

The Story of Joseph

The story of Joseph, son of Jacob, is a stirring illustration of what the Lord will do for those who patiently wait upon him. Favored by his father, resented and hated by his brothers, crisis became the very pattern of Joseph's life: thrown into a pit by his brothers to die (but rescued from that fate by the merciful Judah), sold into slavery, falsely accused of sexual assault, years spent in prison for a crime he did not commit.

But finally, in God's timing, Joseph found favor with Pharaoh, king of Egypt; being placed second in command over the entire kingdom as a reward for his interpretation of Pharaoh's dream and the building of silos to store food for the seven years of famine that were to come after seven years of plenty.

Throughout all of his ordeals, Joseph quietly endured, with the blessing of God upon him, even as the dreams of his youth had foretold. One of the most touching stories in all of the Bible is the account of Joseph's brothers coming to Egypt in search of food, for the famine had reached even as far away as Canaan.

After many meetings in which his brothers did not recognize him, and he did not reveal his identity, Joseph finally told them who he was. The brothers were surely filled with fear, certain that Joseph would exact vengeance for their selling him into slavery and allowing Jacob to believe that his favorite son had been killed by a wild animal. But instead, Joseph loudly wept and said, "But now, do not therefore be grieved or angry with yourselves because you sold me here; for God sent me before you to preserve life" (Genesis 45:5).

And again, later, after Jacob had died and they feared that Joseph would surely then repay them for their treachery:

> 'But as for you, you meant evil against me; but God meant it for good, in order to bring it about as it is this day, to save many people alive. Now therefore, do not be afraid; I will provide for you and your little ones.' And he comforted them and spoke kindly to them.
>
> Genesis 50:20–21

Joseph's reactions to the difficult circumstances of his life were truly Christ-like and a model for us to note no matter what might happen to us; we must rest in the arrangements that come forth from the hand of God, humbling ourselves, knowing that in due time, He will lift us up. Joseph was living proof that things do work together for the good of those who love God, to those who are called according to his promise. Hallelujah!

Moses and the Coming of the Law

The children of Israel remained in Egypt for over four hundred years after the days of Joseph. For a time, for the sake of Joseph, they were highly favored in the land; but then a new Pharaoh came into power, and the Israelites became the slaves of Egypt. Enter Moses; for it was he who was chosen by God to be the deliverer of his people.

Due to fear of the burgeoning number of children born to Hebrew women, the king passed an edict that all male children of the Israelites be thrown into the river and drowned. By the wisdom and cleverness of his mother and sister, however, the life of baby Moses was saved. Not only did the daughter of Pharaoh find Moses floating in the ark of bulrushes that day and have compassion on him, taking him into the house of her father, but Moses' mother, Jochebed, was hired to nurse him!

As the adopted son of Pharaoh's daughter, Moses grew up in the palace of the king. He watched as his people were cruelly treated by the Egyptians (for surely he must have known that the Hebrews were his kinsmen). One day, seeing a slave being mistreated by his master, Moses rose up and slew the Egyptian, burying him in the sand. Of course it was not long before Pharaoh learned of the crime, and Moses had to flee for his life. By his natural strength, Moses had attempted to help his people, but the Lord God had other plans and did not allow Moses to succeed.

As a fugitive, Moses hid out in the Midianite desert for forty years. He chose a wife from one of the seven daughters of the priest of Midian, had a family, and seemingly forgot all about his former life. But all the while, the Spirit of the Lord was working on God's chosen instrument, breaking him down, ridding him of pride and natural strength. Finally, one day he was ready for the mission of the Lord.

At the burning bush, when God called him to his ministry, Moses had become so meek and unsure of himself that it took divine persuasion, and many signs from God, to enlist his man. But this is precisely the point; it took these very qualities for God to be able to use Moses. In Numbers 12:3, it declares this about the Lord's servant: "Now the man Moses was very humble, more than all men who were on the face of the earth."

The necessary meekness had been worked into Moses for the task ahead, a task that would require obedience, endurance, and absolute faith in whatever God said was the course to take.

By the miraculous deliverance from Egypt, God substantiated all He had spoken to His servant. Next came the wilderness testing. But what should have taken approximately eleven days took forty years to accomplish! The long delay was caused by the fleshly, soulish ways of the Israelites; they simply could not wait upon the Lord and trust Him to take them safely into the promised land.

As a result, all who had left Egypt died, except Joshua and Caleb and the children born during the desert sojourn. Even Moses, who failed to sanctify God when he struck the rock a second time to bring forth water, instead of speaking to it, was not allowed to enter Canaan. That particular day, God was not angered by the people's demand for water, so when Moses spoke forth in anger when he struck the rock, he misrepresented God; he did not separate his own feelings from those of the Lord.

When first becoming a believer and reading this story, I was overwhelmed by God's judgment. Here was a man who had endured the reviling and rebellion of his people for almost four decades, and for one transgression, he was to be excluded from crossing the Jordan into Canaan! I thought to myself at the time, *Then what is the use for me even trying to do the will of God if a man such as Moses failed? How harsh God is.*

But in time, I began to understand. To he who is given much, much is required, the Scripture says; and certainly Moses was granted tremendous intimacy and authority with God. Likewise, the Word says that not many should desire to be teachers, for they shall be more strictly judged. This is for the same reason: in order to truly teach, God must release much in the way of revelation, making all teachers highly responsible for the very things they are teaching.

The ways of the Lord are indeed always just.

And what a man Moses turned out to be. Not only did he humbly accept his fate, he sang a song to the Lord! It was a song of praise and teaching, proclaiming the greatness of the Lord and the perfection of all His ways. He reminded the people of their errant ways and the gracious way God had dealt with them. He recounted all their rebellion in detail; but then, as in so many of the psalms of David, their creator's mercy and compassion broke forth once the people had cried out to Him in repentance:

> For the Lord will judge His people and have compassion on His servants, when He sees that their power is gone, and there is no one remaining, bond or free... He will provide atonement for the land and His people.
>
> Deuteronomy 32:36, 43b

Of course, long before the crossing into Canaan, Moses had received the commandments of God, what we commonly call the Law of Moses. The people still did not know that they could never find a way back to a holy God in the condition they were in, by simply doing things that would please Him. God knew, but they did not.

So He gave them the Law for that very purpose: for them to see their inability to meet the standards necessary to even directly approach God, much less to abide in His presence. The elaborate system of sacrifices and ordinances did allow the people some access to the throne of His mercy, to serve its purpose, and then pass away. But even under the Law, the history of the Hebrew nation was one long series of bell-shaped curves of progress and failure, of rebellion followed by brief periods of repentance and revival.

The long history of the kings and priests, prophets, and holy men, as well as that of the common people themselves, continued to bear the tragic marks of mankind's fallen condition. After periods of repentance, the Lord would renew His blessings; but the people in their prosperity would forget God, which would cause the cycle to repeat itself again and again.

Of course, a Savior, a Messiah, had been foretold by the prophets, one who would rescue the people from their bondage, once and for all, and lead them into a permanent place of safety and holiness: the most high would be their God, and they would be His people; and all the promises made to Abraham, Isaac, and Jacob would at long last be theirs.

So, rather than recounting any more of the tragic sagas of fallen man, even God's own chosen people, all the highs and lows, let us move forward to the "fullness of time" and God's answer to the situation, the birth of Jesus. Without this great intervention by the Father, there would be no way back to God, and His eternal purpose would have been impossible.

PART TWO:
GOD'S ETERNAL PLAN
THE COMING OF CHRIST

> But when the fullness of time had come, God sent forth His Son, born of a woman, born under the law, to redeem those who were under the law, that we might receive the adoption of sons.
>
> Galatians 4:4

The Word declares that it was in the "fullness of time" that Jesus came forth; time and history had ripened to critical mass in God's eyes. It was time for His solution to sin to manifest itself: the seed of the woman who would crush the serpent's head (Genesis 3:15) was born.

It is extremely important to understand that Jesus came as a man, born under the Law. The first Adam had given man's dominion away, and it required the coming of the second Adam to restore that dominion. Regardless of what Satan and fallen man had done to thwart it, the eternal purpose and plan of God could not be destroyed.

In coming to earth and defeating the enemy, Christ twice humbled Himself: first by emptying Himself of all the glory He had enjoyed with the Father from eternity past and coming as one of us; and secondly by humbling Himself as a man to God in perfect obedience, even unto death on the cross.

The four gospels chronicle His life, death, and resurrection, but each from a different point of view: in Matthew, He came as King; in Mark, as the suffering servant; in Luke, as the perfect man; and in John, as God. Certain events are repeated in all four books, but each account has its own unique character and overall theme.

It is the book of Matthew on which we will spend most of our time, for I believe it has been greatly misunderstood, with many essential truths that the work of the enemy has been able to hide. Since Matthew announces the coming of the King and His Kingdom, its contents are a direct threat and frontal attack on the kingdom of darkness Satan has established upon the earth; hence the enemy's counterattack on this portion of the Word. By deception he has been able to persuade most believers that Matthew is pretty much the same as the other three gospels, just another account of the life and death of Jesus. Such an understanding misses Matthew's main point: The Kingdom is at hand!

Matthew is the first book of the New Testament, even as Genesis is the first of the Old, and as such it contains the seeds of all that follows between itself and the book of Revelation, and serves as a vital link between the two covenants. The eternal purpose of God is to sum up all things in His Son, so that Christ might be all-in-all; that purpose has never changed.

To accomplish His purpose, two problems had to be overcome: the rebellion of Lucifer and the fall of man. Christ is the solution to both problems: His perfect life as a man born of woman, and His sacrificial death on the cross as atonement for all who believe, has defeated Satan and sin once and for all. The law of sin and death has been overcome by the law of the Spirit of Life (Romans 8:2).

And by indwelling the spirit of man with His own Life (for He is a Life-giving Spirit), He has enabled the sons of men to overcome the enemy even as He did. Not through works of the flesh, but by Christ Himself, living His Life out through these vessels of clay.

Let us go now to the book of Matthew where it was announced by John the Baptist:

> "Repent, for the kingdom of Heaven is at hand!"
>
> Matthew 3:2

With the help of the Holy Spirit, let us see if we can discover exactly what is meant by that incredible declaration. First, however, there is much to be gleaned from the genealogy and birth of Jesus.

THE GENEALOGY OF JESUS

Matthew 1:1–17

Every detail of the life, ministry, and death of Jesus is extremely important to notice. Even his genealogy is of paramount significance. Who is this Man? Where did He come from? We know that as the Christ of God, He has no beginning and no end; but as the Son of Man, his origins are critical, for all the prophetic words spoken concerning His advent and purpose must be seen as fulfilled beyond dispute.

Since in the book of Matthew, Jesus came as King, His genealogy must be traced in royal fashion. Hence He is spoken of as the "Son of David" (v. 1), and many more kings are a part of His family line. But He also came as a man, the son of Abraham, through Judah, therefore, the promised Messiah to the Hebrew nation. In this line, five women are mentioned along the way, a very unusual development (one worthy of further study and consideration), for the Jewish people traditionally traced their ancestry through the males only.

The five women are Tamar, Rahab, Ruth, the wife of Uriah (Bathsheba), and Mary, the mother of Jesus. When we examine the lives of the first four, something very interesting develops:

Tamar was a woman who sinned and then justified it; Rahab was a prostitute who had faith in the living God; Ruth was a Moabitess who found redemption marrying Boaz, the kinsman redeemer; and Bathsheba was a great sinner, but once saved, she never left the house of David again, even giving birth to Solomon, David's successor as king of Israel.

So, the facts worth noting here are these: We have a sinner (Tamar), very much like ourselves. We have a second sinner (Rahab), but one who had faith in God, whose faith not only saved her from being destroyed at Jericho but also gave her the privilege of being a maternal ancestor of Jesus Himself. In Ruth we find a woman outside the promised people of God, a Gentile, who found redemption by being "grafted" in as it were by faith; and in Bathsheba, we find a woman of great sin who was also taken into the house of God, and once forgiven, never left it again.

All were sinners saved by grace, as are we, and the pattern of their salvation is an image of our own: sinner, faith, redemption, and eternal security; and all four women were remarried women, even as we are married for the second time, becoming the Bride of Christ.

But in Mary, there is a distinct difference. She does not belong with the other four in a sense. For she was chosen to be the mother of Christ, who was to become the seed of the woman who would crush the serpent's head (Gen. 3:15). Throughout forty-two generations, women had come and gone, even the four mentioned above, but none of them fulfilled the prophecy of the promised seed. Mary alone fulfilled the prophecy perfectly.

The forty-two generations are divided into three groups of fourteen generations each. Numbers in the Scriptures always have some significance, but we must be careful to interpret them correctly and not place too much importance on them.

But we should take note that forty is often the number associated with testing (it took the children of Israel forty years to reach Canaan once they were delivered from Egypt; during the

Great Flood it rained for forty days and nights; Jesus fasted for forty days during His trial in the wilderness). In each case, testing also had judgment attached to it.

Two is the number of testimony or witness (the testimony of the two spies who gave a good report when they spied out the land; it took the testimony of two witnesses to condemn a man in criminal cases), so forty-two can be seen as a perfect testimony that during forty generations of testing, mankind failed to produce the promised seed of the woman, for such was the judgment of God.

Fourteen can be seen in one of two ways: as seven times two, or ten plus four. Seven is one of the perfect numbers of God, so coupled with the testimony of the number two, we can see that there is a perfect testimony, repeated three times (three being a number of completeness, as the Father, Son, and Holy Spirit being the Godhead). Hence a complete and perfect testimony of the conclusion we reached in the paragraph above: mankind's failure to produce the woman God had ordained to bear the precious seed.

In the combination of ten plus four to make fourteen, ten is also often a number connected with testing (as the church at Smyrna in Revelations 2:8–11 passing through tribulation for ten days). Four is the number associated with created things (the four living creatures in Heaven represent created things; on earth there are four main directions, the four elements of earth, sky, wind, and fire, etc.)

So three cycles of fourteen generations each had been tested by God, from Abraham to Christ, but none had brought forth the promised seed; it was not until the end of the third cycle that Mary appeared, and God Himself fathered the man Jesus. The promised seed had finally arrived!

All the above, and I am sure much more, can be gleaned from a careful consideration of the genealogy of our Lord and Savior, all of which causes us to bow and worship in great wonder and adoration!

Mark gives no genealogy for the Lord, the reason being that in Mark, he came as the suffering servant, and servants have no genealogy of any real importance. In Luke, He came as the perfect man, so a genealogy is given: one that traces Jesus back to Adam, for the Lord was indeed a man, even the second man and last Adam (1 Cor. 15:47). In the book of John, Jesus is presented as God, and God has no beginning and no end, therefore no genealogy.

The precision of the Word of God is truly a marvelous thing!

THE BIRTH OF JESUS

> Now after Jesus was born in Bethlehem of Judea in the days of Herod the king, behold, wise men from the East came to Jerusalem, saying, 'Where is He who was born King of the Jews? For we have seen His star in the East and have come to worship Him.'
>
> Matthew 2:1–2

In the sovereign will of God, the time had come to send His only begotten Son into the world for the purpose of salvation and restoration: He would save men from their sins and separation from God and restore the dominion given to mankind at the time of his creation. With the Life and glory of Christ indwelling man, Satan and his fallen host would be defeated and judged, and His Son would finally be all-in-all and the sum of all things. The door to God's eternal purpose would be opened by the birth of Jesus, but the road ahead would still be a steep and rugged one.

The circumstances surrounding the birth of Jesus are quite interesting and revealing. First of all, it was Gentiles who knew beforehand that the Savior, for whom the Jews had been waiting, had been born. It seems that in their study of astronomy, a star appeared (the star mentioned by Balaam in Numbers 24:17?). But it had to be God who revealed to them the significance of the star.

The Jews, on the other hand, knew nothing about the star, and did not even go out to see for themselves what the strangers were talking about. They knew the letter of the Law, the scribes quickly answering where the Messiah was to be born, but they were completely devoid of the Spirit (2 Corinthians 3:6).

When the wise men finally arrived in Bethlehem, they worshiped the "young Child," not the babe; for by this time, both the parents and Jesus were living in a house and not in the stable where the baby had been born. So the popular nativity scene depicting the wise men, shepherds, animals, and parents in a stable is completely inaccurate. Time had passed between the birth and the arrival of the wise men with their gifts of gold, frankincense, and myrrh.

These three gifts were highly significant as well, although it is doubtful that the wise men understood their meaning: gold signifies the divine nature of God; frankincense a fragrant and well-pleasing life unto God; and myrrh is symbolic of death and burial. So this King, whom they had come to see and worship, was to possess the glory of God Himself. He would live a perfect life before the Father, and finally, would die a victorious death, freeing people from the bondage of sin, death, and judgment.

Joseph, an honorable and obedient man, was warned in a dream by an angel to flee to Egypt. For King Herod would soon pass his edict that all male children under the age of two years were to be killed. Joseph immediately obeyed, and the holy family sojourned in Egypt until Joseph was instructed to return to Israel. This revelation also came by way of a dream, informing the earthly father of Jesus that King Herod was dead. Again Joseph obeyed, the family returned to Israel and settled in Nazareth.

Nazareth was such an unlikely place for a king to dwell, being an area that was despised by the Jews, located in the Galilee of the Gentiles. Both of these points seem inherently prophetic: for Christ Himself would be despised by a majority of the Jews, and the Gentiles were to be the ones who would come to the Lord in the greatest numbers, from that day down until the time of the Gentiles is fulfilled.

THE GOSPEL OF THE KINGDOM

In those days John the Baptist came preaching in the wilderness of Judea, and saying, 'Repent, for the kingdom of Heaven is at hand!

Matthew 3:1–2

From that time Jesus began to preach and to say, "Repent, for the kingdom of Heaven is at hand.

Matthew 4:17

And this gospel of the kingdom will be preached in all the world as a witness to all the nations, and then the end will come.

Matthew 24:14

The above quotes are critical to understanding that the book of Matthew is the book of the Kingdom. The Kingdom is foremost in the mind of God; His Kingdom coming to the earth that He might reign here even as He does in Heaven. Somehow the idea of the church has taken precedence over the Kingdom. This even though the Kingdom is presented more than fifty times in Matthew, and Jesus mentioned the church twice!

It is not the church that builds the Kingdom, but rather the Kingdom that builds the church. For the Kingdom has come when the King is present and ruling. Without the King there is no Kingdom, and without the Kingdom there is no church. All the emphasis in Matthew is on the Kingdom, which we are told by Christ to seek *first*. John the Baptist came announcing it, Jesus preached it, as did the early apostles and disciples.

The eternal purpose of God is intimately connected to the Kingdom, of course: for until Christ is all-in-all, the Kingdom remains limited, present only in certain individual hearts, those who have made the Lord absolutely sovereign and the sum of all things in their lives. This connection is a key truth that must be recovered and lived by the church if we are to see the Kingdom come.

John the Baptist was the first to proclaim the coming of the Kingdom. Let's take a look now at this great prophet and forerunner of Christ, and what he had to say regarding the King and His Kingdom.

JOHN THE BAPTIST

> For this is he who was spoken of by the prophet Isaiah, saying: "The voice of one crying in the wilderness: 'Prepare the way of Lord; make His paths straight.'"
>
> Matthew 3:3; Isaiah 40:3

The forerunner of the Lord came with a single message: "Repent, for the kingdom of Heaven is at hand!" (Matthew 3:2). John came to prepare the way of the Lord, by announcing that all men were sinners and in need of repentance, and that One was on His way to save them from their sins.

Upon first becoming a believer, I was troubled by this declaration by John. If the Kingdom of Heaven was at hand, where had it gone, and why are we still here two thousand years later? I had been taught and thought of Heaven in both geographical and temporal terms; that someday we will go to a place called Heaven, hence a specific place where Heaven is located and a particular time in which those saved by Christ will go and dwell with Him forever. Is this what the Baptist was announcing?

Many years have passed since my misconception concerning Heaven, and I have come to a different understanding of what John was saying. Certainly there is a place called Heaven, and one day we will dwell there forever with the Lord. But this is not what John the Baptist was proclaiming those days in the Judean desert.

The Kingdom of Heaven indeed was "at hand" when John declared it; it was at hand because the King who was bringing it was at hand. And who was that King? The man Jesus, who would only do, say, or think what He heard from the Father, giving God absolute rule over His life and death.

The term "Kingdom" occurs in three different ways when being referred to in a spiritual context in Scripture: the Kingdom of God, which is above time and space, stretching from eternity past to eternity future, and where the rule and sovereignty of God are unchallenged and absolute; the Kingdom of Heaven, the domain brought to earth by Jesus, and the Millennial Kingdom, the thousand-year reign of Christ and His overcomers, on the earth, and yet in the future.

Satan had rebelled and man had fallen; the absolute rule of God had been breached. Therefore, it became necessary for God to send His Son, bearing the Kingdom of Heaven, to live a life of total obedience unto God, and by so doing, to make a way for the Father to once again rule the earth as well as the Heavens.

So the Kingdom of Heaven is not merely a matter of time and space; rather it is any time and in any place that the Kingdom of God rules. It first so ruled in Jesus, who in turn has placed it in us, that the Kindom of God might rule supreme in our lives, even as it did in Christ's.

The Millennial Kingdom is for those overcomers who have allowed this process to take place in their lives: spirit has become the regent of their lives (directed and empowered by the Holy Spirit); soul has become the faithful steward of the spirit, with the body following the dictates received from God.

The overcomers spoken of in Revelation 2 and 3 have not only overcome sin, but have also overcome self. Self has forever been man's problem, from the rebellion in Eden even to the present day. Perhaps this diagram will better explain what I am trying to say:

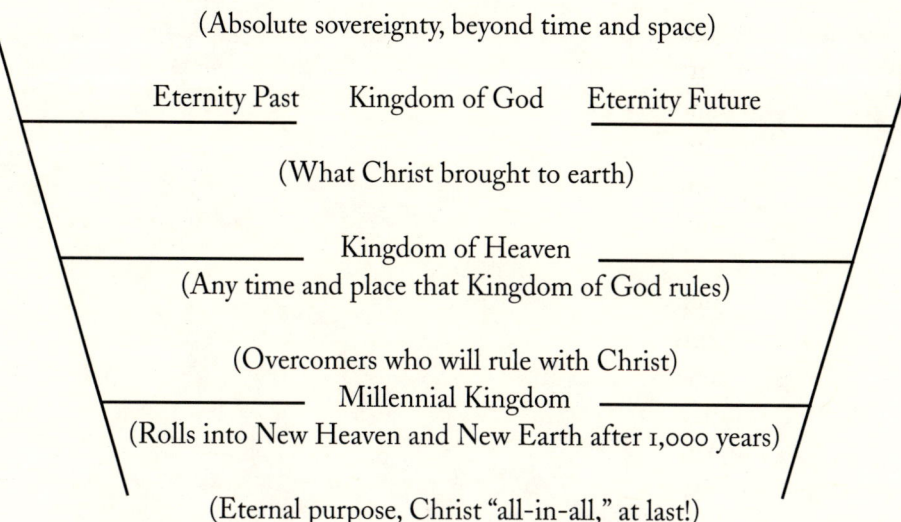

This is the gospel of the Kingdom, first spoken by John the Baptist, repeated by Christ once He began His ministry, and the same gospel of the early disciples and apostles. And this is the gospel referred to in Matt. 24:14: "And this gospel of the kingdom will be preached in all the world as a witness to all nations, and then the end will come."

The gospel of the Kingdom includes more than individual salvation. Personal reconciliation with God is a gift of grace, what God has done for us. The gospel of the Kingdom is what we are to do for God. He saved us that we might live for Him by the implanted Life of Christ, and thereby have our part in bringing about the eternal purpose of God. To die not only to sin, but to self, that He might reign supreme in our lives.

Certainly one must be saved, but we are saved from this kingdom into His Kingdom: the realm where God rules, unimpeded by any part of His creation, so that Christ might be the sum of all things. This is the good news!

TRUE REPENTANCE

Ask most people what repentance means, and they will say to be sorry for the things they have done against the will of God, the many sins they have committed; some will even add that it also includes turning from those transgressions and living a life of obedience to God. This is all true enough, but again only a half-truth.

True repentance means that there is no hope for me whatsoever; I altogether deserve nothing but judgment and death. Everything about me is wrong; there is no fixing me up through self-improvement (or even improvement by God). All my works are as filthy rags to God. We sin because of who and what we are; *we* are the problem. The sins are only the natural outworking of that problem, symptoms of the disease.

This is what John the Baptist preached. His baptism was a baptism of death, not the baptism of salvation, for Christ had not yet been delivered up. The baptism that would follow after the death and resurrection of our Lord is a baptism of death and a baptism into Life, signifying that the old man has died and the new man in Christ has been born. But death of the whole being is necessary if new Life is to manifest itself. None of our natural qualities are salvageable; not just the "bad" ones but also none of the "good" ones. They both must go, indeed *we* must go. This is true repentance.

The problem is that we have been taught and accepted a form of false easy-beliefism: just be sorry for our sins and believe in Jesus and we are saved. Unknowingly, we bring a large part of our old self into our walk with the Lord. Our soul is still mostly in charge of our life; instead of continuing in sin, we reason, we will learn to walk in the way of the Lord. But such a walk is impossible so long as we still make most of the decisions in our life, even the way in which we will worship God.

Such a life is doomed to failure and frustration, and the kingdom of darkness remains alive and well. Some of the tares planted by the evil one were expressly for that purpose, to spawn "some other" gospel, which is no gospel at all.

THE BAPTISM OF JESUS

> Then Jesus came from Galilee to John at the Jordan to be baptized by him. And John tried to prevent Him, saying, 'I need to be baptized by You, and are You coming to me?' But Jesus answered and said to him, 'Permit it to be so now, for thus it is fitting for us to fulfill all righteousness.' Then he allowed Him.
>
> Matthew 3:13–15

> When He had been baptized, Jesus came up immediately from the water; and behold, the Heavens were opened to Him, and He saw the Spirit of God descending like a dove and alighting upon Him. And suddenly a voice came from Heaven, saying, 'This is My beloved Son, in whom I am well pleased.'
>
> Matthew 3:16–17

At least three things stand out in the account of the baptism of Jesus: John's reaction and Jesus's answer to John, Jesus being baptized by the Holy Spirit as well as by water, and the Father's announcement and seal of approval. This was to be the beginning of the Lord's ministry, so it is critical that we understand the significance of these points. Up to that time, so far as we know, Jesus had not done any ministering. Between the ages of twelve and thirty, the Bible is silent about the life of the Lord. But after His baptisms, that was all about to change.

John was taken aback when Jesus came to be baptized. He is the Lamb of God that taketh away the sins of the world, the Baptist must have reasoned, so why is He here to be baptized by me? Jesus answered that it must be so, for all righteousness to be fulfilled. Certainly it was not because Jesus had sinned, so why was it fitting to do so? What did Jesus mean by His answer?

If we remember that Jesus came as a man on behalf of mankind to stand in the place of man, then it makes total sense. Man had sinned and become separated from God. Jesus came to represent fallen man's condition. Therefore as that representative it was proper, even necessary, that He too be baptized.

It was also to show that all of the Lord's work was to be done on the ground of resurrection; for baptism is more than just having one's sins forgiven. It is also death of the old man and the resurrection of the new; the old man is drowned in the waters of baptism, and the new man is resurrected to new Life upon the coming up out of the water. Only that which passes through death and comes out on the other side is of any value to God.

Jesus not only was baptized by John that day, but He was also baptized by the Holy Spirit, who descended like a dove and lighted upon the Lord. This was the anointing of God for the work that lay ahead. And with that anointing came the Father's seal of approval. We know very little about the details of the Lord's life from birth to the age of thirty, but the words that boomed from Heaven that day tell us all that we need to know: everything about the Lord, every thought, word, and deed was approved by God as perfect and worthy for the work of redemption.

Of course those words would be contested by Satan, even as the words of God after the creation of man were challenged. Such is the way of our enemy. He will always attempt to refute or thwart the Word of God.

THE WILDERNESS TESTING

> Then Jesus was led up by the Spirit into the wilderness to be tempted by the devil. And when He had fasted forty days and forty nights, afterward He was hungry.
>
> Matthew 4:1–2

Satan will always come and test any movement toward God; this was true in the life of the Lord, and it is true in ours. In the case of Jesus, it was the Spirit Himself who led the Lord into the wilderness to be tempted and tried by the devil. Satan waited until Jesus was weakened by forty days of fasting before he moved in to begin his deceptions (he always seems to show up in our weakest moments).

The first Adam had been tested in a perfect environment, surrounded by food, with a helpmate, and with the presence of God nearby. The last Adam was tried in a desert place, with nothing to eat, and the Father had withdrawn Himself and removed all hedges of protection, leaving Jesus alone to test His Son's total dependence on the Father.

There is no way to truly understand Matthew 4 without going back to Genesis 3 and comparing and contrasting the two temptations. The first Adam committed two grave offenses that day in Eden: by eating the forbidden fruit, he declared his independence from God, and he stepped over from his blessed position as man, created in the image and likeness of God, to that of being as god himself, rebelling against the authority of his Creator.

God is willing to share everything with man except His Deity, for it is written:

> Grace and peace be multiplied to you in the knowledge of God and of Jesus our Lord, as His divine power has given to us all things that pertain to life and godliness; through the knowledge of Him who has called us by glory and virtue, by which have been given to us exceedingly great and precious promises, that through these you may be partakers of the divine nature, having escaped the corruption that is in the world through lust.
>
> 2 Peter 1:2–4

Please note: *partakers,* but never as God ourselves.

Jesus, on the other hand, who indeed is God, would not act independently of the Father, and refused to leave his position as man; for if He had responded to Satan's temptations as God, and not man, we would have no salvation today. Of course, because He was totally under the authority of God, He could do many miracles by that authority, even as is possible for believers today. But He never took the position of God, which is what Satan tempted Him to do in the first two temptations. Jesus refused and remained in His place as a man. Do you see the difference?

Satan will always come to dispute the Word of God: the beginning of the temptation of Eve was opened by this question, "Did God say…?" Likewise, after hearing the Father from Heaven declare that indeed Jesus is His beloved Son, in whom He is well pleased, Satan repeated the same tactic with the words, "*If* You are the Son of God…" In both cases, the veracity of God was questioned, so as to make room for the insertion of deception. We must be vigilant ourselves, knowing that each step of progress we make in the Life of the Spirit will be tested in the same way.

Jesus must have been near starvation after forty days and forty nights of fasting, so the nature of the first temptation tested his physical need for food. By tempting Jesus to turn the stones into bread, Satan was actually trying to get Christ to prove His Godhood. Could He have turned the stones into bread? Of course He could, but He received no word from the Father to do so, hence He refused.

The Lord also wanted us to see in this temptation that our spiritual well-being far exceeds our need to satisfy the flesh. After all, He has promised that the righteous will never beg for bread; and the first prayer in the Lord's Prayer after praying for the Kingdom and God's will is for the Lord to provide our daily bread and necessary physical provisions.

The second temptation of Satan was aimed at the realm of the soul, especially testing the will of the Lord. Taking him to a high pinnacle of the temple, our foe said:

> If You are the Son of God, throw Yourself down. For it is written: 'He shall give His angels charge over You,' and 'In their hands they shall bear You up, lest you dash Your foot against a stone.'
>
> Matthew 4:5–6

This was a perfect example of Satan's use of Scripture-twisting, quoting the Word for his own purpose of deception. Indeed, these words do appear in Scripture, being a part of the psalm of protection, Psalm 91; but they did not apply in this situation because the Father did not give them nor confirm them.

That is precisely the point of Christ's response:

> Jesus said to him, "It is written again, 'You shall not tempt the Lord your God.'"
>
> Deuteronomy 6:16

Tempt Him to do what? To do something God had not spoken for that moment. So many diligent believers memorize vast tracts of Scripture, which is a good thing because the Word itself admonishes us to do so. But in the midst of a crisis, we must not just pull out and quote a Scripture because it happens to pertain to the situation. The word that is effective is the word the Spirit gives at that instant, not one that emerges from rote memory alone. The Father did not say, "Go ahead, jump." To do so anyway, on the basis of Satan's misuse of Scripture, would have been sin.

In the final temptation, Satan left the possibility of tempting Jesus to prove that He is God. Instead, he appealed to Him on the grounds of being a man. By taking him to a high mountain, showing and offering Him all the kingdoms of the world and their glory, the enemy used his last card, at least for the moment.

Could he have given Christ the kingdoms and their glory? Absolutely, because he is the prince of this world. Would he have done so had Jesus agreed to bow down and worship him? Again, yes, because the one thing Satan has always craved is worship, to be as God. Men who do not know Christ are worshiping Satan, whether they know it or not, but to obtain worship from a good man, even a perfect man, would satisfy Satan's deepest longings. The things of this world, even to Satan, are just things, mere trifles and idols. What he has always really been after is to be worshiped as God.

Of course Jesus refused to do such a foolish thing with this answer: "Away with you, Satan! For it is written, 'You shall worship the Lord your God, and Him only you shall serve.'" (Matthew 4:10, Deuteronomy 6:13).

This was the third time Christ used the book of Deuteronomy to counter the attacks of the enemy. In the first temptation, He quoted Deuteronomy 8:3, and in the second, Deut. 6:16. Was His use of Deuteronomy all three times just a coincidence? Of course not, nothing in Scripture is just a coincidence.

The book of Deuteronomy has as its main theme the subject of obedience, which is what Christ brought back to the earth. It is not that no one had ever obeyed God, for here and there some had. But no one had ever obeyed Him completely, and we know that the Word says that if we fail on even one point, we have failed on all accounts. So by obeying here (as well as for the rest of His life) Jesus reestablished the absolute authority of God upon the earth.

Deuteronomy is also the book of the Law, which Jesus came to obey and satisfy completely so that we might live by His grace. Therefore, the words from Deuteronomy fit the occasion perfectly.

After the third temptation, Satan left Jesus for a season, and the angels came to minister to the Lord. He had passed His trial and testing in the wilderness and shut the enemy's mouth.

THE MINISTRY OF CHRIST BEGINS

> From that time Jesus began to preach, and to say, 'Repent, for the kingdom of Heaven is at hand.'
>
> Matthew 4:17

With the anointing of God fully upon Him, and His defeat of the enemy, Jesus began to preach the same message as John the Baptist: to die to self altogether, and to receive the Kingdom of Heaven within, experiencing both the forgiveness of sins and the empowerment of the Life of Christ living Himself out through the human vessel; the only way to make Christ all-in-all and the sum of all things. This is the gospel of the Kingdom; anything else is a construction of Satan and fallen man.

Jesus also began to call men unto Himself and this gospel. Andrew, then Peter, the two brothers, John and James, dropped everything and followed Him. All four were fishermen, but Jesus beckoned them to a higher calling: "Then He said, 'Follow Me, and I will make you fishers of men'" (Matthew 4:19). Their immediate obedience is something we should carefully note. And the Holy Spirit supported the preaching of Christ by confirming it by great signs and wonders: Jesus healed all kinds of sickness and torments, and delivered the demon-possessed.

THE SERMON ON THE MOUNT

> And seeing the multitudes, He went up on a mountain, and when He was seated His disciples came to Him. Then He opened His mouth and taught them, saying...
>
> Matthew 5:1

Jesus's fame had spread throughout all Syria. His healing of the sick and demon- possessed attracted vast crowds. Seeing the multitudes, He decided to take His disciples aside and teach them the deeper truths of the Kingdom.

I do not believe that the teaching on the Mount was for the multitudes that day, for they represent the world. And I do not believe the teaching describes the manner of living in the future Kingdom, thereby excusing us from its demands today. The Kingdom will be the reward of those who live by the principles Jesus taught that day; all who will rule and reign with Christ during the Millennium must live by those Kingdom standards *now, today,* during each man's earthly sojourn.

In the Scriptures, elevation is often a symbol of higher living, so by taking the disciples up on a mountain, the idea of living spiritually above the commonplace is suggested. The Sermon on the Mount is the very essence of the teaching of Christ. And those who live in this way are one and the same as the overcomers of Revelation, chapters 2 and 3; and the wise virgins of Matthew 25: these are they who will have paid the price of death to self and given themselves over to wanting nothing but the glory of God. For such as these, the Kingdom of Heaven is *now*, for their character has become that of the Master, who has become to them all-in-all and the sum of all things.

The first several verses of Matthew 5 have become known as the Beatitudes, which means the state of utmost bliss. Ultimate happiness has been found by those who live in this way, for they have found who they really are. Most live out their lives thinking of themselves in a certain way, the way their sin, life's circumstances, and Satan have molded them into thinking. How many times have you heard someone say, "That's just the way I am"?

It is this false self that man struggles so to keep, not knowing there is anything else. But it is by giving up this false idea of self-hood that one finds his true self, the one God has created and ordained him to be (Matthew 10:39). Such a discovery and such a life *is* the source of utmost bliss.

The Poor in Spirit

> "Blessed are the poor in spirit, for theirs is the kingdom of Heaven."
>
> Matthew 5:3

Who are the poor in spirit? Does this blessing have anything to do with money and worldly wealth? Are situations other than monetary ones covered by this verse? The answers to these questions have been many. To say the poor in spirit has nothing to do with Mammon does not square with Luke's version of the Beatitudes: "Blessed are you poor, for yours is the kingdom of Heaven" (Luke 6:20).

Luke leaves out the words "in spirit" and seems to be quoting Jesus's words to actual poor people. But by including "in spirit," Matthew's quotation covers a broader range of possibilities.

The fact that this verse is the first of the Beatitudes is significant. We all must realize that we are bankrupt when it comes to spiritual matters; even our spirits are worthless to us if they are not filled, guided, and empowered by the Holy Spirit. This destitution of the spirit is what necessitates our total dependence on God.

With this fact firmly in place, all the other Beatitudes and teachings of Christ become possible, for it is not us but the Life of Christ that enables us to follow them. This is true in all areas of our life, even in the use of money and worldly possessions.

What is to be our attitude toward Mammon? We know we are not to worship it, and we know that the love of money is a root of all kinds of evil (1 Timothy 6:10); and furthermore, that it is harder for a rich man to enter Heaven than for a camel to pass through the eye of a needle (Matthew 19:24). And yet we do have to handle money as part of our life in this world.

But in fact, when we really think about it, money itself, monetary value placed on everything, is a creation of Satan. With God, all is by His marvelous grace, even eternal Life. But Satan has always trafficked in everything, even the bodies and souls of men (Revelation 18:13). So although we must use it in this world, money is something that must be handled very carefully, for when we touch it, we touch the enemy.

So in the final analysis, what is to be our attitude toward wealth? Who fails the test of being "poor in spirit" when it comes to money? Proverbs 30, called the wisdom of Agur, offers some insight on this question:

> Give me neither poverty nor riches—feed me with the food allotted to me; lest I be full and deny You, and say, 'Who is the Lord?' Or lest I be poor and steal, and profane the name of my God.
>
> Proverbs 30:8–9

From this Word, it seems that both the rich and poor, materially speaking, can fail to be poor in spirit: the rich because they will forget God, depending upon riches in His place; and the poor because they may steal and profane the name of God due to their lack. So to be poor in spirit is to be satisfied with what the Lord has allotted for us, to neither complain if we are poor, nor crave for more or depend on our wealth if we be rich. Paul put it this way:

> Not that I speak in regard to need, for I have learned in whatever state I am, to be content: I know how to be abased, and I know how to abound. Everywhere and in all things I have learned both to be full and to be hungry, both to abound and to suffer need.
>
> Philippians 4:11–12

One final word needs to be spoken on this matter of wealth and the use of money.

So-called "prosperity preaching" has become popular in our time. I find this doctrine contrary to the Word of God and deeply offensive. Our Savior was born in a stable, was buried in a borrowed tomb, and while He was upon this earth, by His own Words, "had no place to lay His Head" (Luke 9:58).

So, how can we desire after riches and luxury when the Lord had none? We are enjoined to follow after Him who had nothing and expected nothing from this world. We are therefore to live likewise, which negates the whole premise of prosperity preaching.

And to depend on the "transference of wealth" from the wicked to the righteous also rests on shaky grounds. The true gospel has such power and vitality that it need not depend on money to proclaim itself. It is true that the children of Israel were given gold and precious things when they left Egypt, but for what did they use it? To build the golden calf! So many well-meaning leaders today have fallen to the same temptation and sin.

Those Who Mourn

"Blessed are those who mourn, for they shall be comforted."

Matthew 5:4

Certainly the world in which we live is a place of great sadness, and when we find ourselves pulled into its clutches, we should be greatly saddened. I suppose this verse is speaking about both of those situations, but I believe the Lord is mainly speaking about all of fallen creation the way God sees it. Compared to what He had in mind, and what existed for a while in Eden, the present earth is surely a deformed place of darkness. Evil abounds, being called good, and goodness is called evil. There is innocent blood shed everywhere: from the unthinkable acts of abortion, senseless and random killings, to wars and rumors of war throughout the earth.

Fallen man has truly become as depraved as Satan himself, the two of them building a kingdom that hates anything that has to do with God and righteousness. Christ died that a Kingdom, even more magnificent than Eden, might be born; but sinful man refuses to submit and receive it. This is surely reason to mourn.

We mourn because we love, whether it be for a loved one who has died or a lost way of life. The deepest and highest mourning, though, is to mourn for what God Himself mourns. Jesus wept at the tomb of Lazarus, surely not for his old friend's death alone, for He was about to raise him from the dead. No, He wept for the human condition, for the sadness of the world and its people brought on by sin and death and how long it would be before all the tragedy and heartbreak would come to an end.

The Father is touched by such mourning, and its reward will be great in Heaven. As our eyes are opened to the heart of the Father, a great burden should fall upon us, to pray and mourn for the things that mean most to Him; and for the Kingdom to come. For when it does, there will be no reason for mourning again; praise His Holy name forever!

The Meek

"Blessed are the meek, for they shall inherit the earth" (Matthew 5:5).

Meekness is a greatly misunderstood character trait. It is most related to the virtue of humility. In this fallen world, it is seen as weakness. Indeed it is power and pride that seem to win the day in our present life. The meek are usually pushed aside as ineffectual weaklings who will not fight and therefore deserve nothing. But these are the very ones who will inherit the earth, Christ said, so there must be something hidden here for us to discover.

We know that Moses was chosen by God to deliver His people from Egypt because at that time, he was the meekest man upon the earth. But it had taken forty years on the backside of the desert, being reduced little-by-little, for him to reach that state. Lacking all confidence in himself and his own strength, Moses was ready for the task at hand.

Obedience by ones such as this is not so difficult. They know they must depend on God alone if anything is to be accomplished. Moses was indeed so meek that the Lord had to "build him up" and convince him that he *could* truly answer God's calling.

Jesus was the epitome of meekness, never depending on Himself but only upon God alone. This was the very source of His authority and power. And He invited us to come to Him and allow Him to be our Life. If we do, meekness will be part of what comes forth from us as "naturally" as pride does now.

True meekness cannot come by any other means. We may try hard to be meek in any situation, and even seem to be enjoying some success; but God will eventually arrange circumstances in which pride and anger will burst out. Meekness is not a virtue that can be produced by merely deciding to be meek and working hard with willpower to bring it about.

True meekness has many qualities; to name a few:

- Meekness makes no demands on others and demands nothing for self: for self has been consigned to the cross and crucified. (Romans 6:6)
- Meekness accepts whatever comes from the hand of God, whether it be blessing or suffering: praise to God arises in all circumstances.
- A meek person is a teachable person: knowing he has no answers himself, he relies upon God.
- Meekness and ever-ready obedience are closely linked; one who is meek does not trust himself, therefore will readily obey what the Spirit of God indicates.
- Meek ones are willing to pick up their crosses daily, knowing that even Jesus learned obedience by the things which He suffered.
- And the truly meek will find the "rest" spoken of in Hebrews 4, for they will mix the Word with faith, knowing that whatever the Lord does or says is completely trustworthy, hence there is no need to be anxious about anything (1 Peter 5:7).

When Jesus said, "Come learn of me, for I am meek and lowly..." (Matthew 11:29), He did not mean to take lessons in how to be meek, but to learn the source of His own meekness, even to be fully submitted to His Life within us, as He was to the Father's. If all things are to be summed up in Christ, and He is to be all-in-all, meekness is included! There is nothing outside Him: *He* is meekness; this is what must be learned.

Spiritual Hunger and Thirst

> Blessed are those who hunger and thirst for righteousness, for they shall be filled.
>
> Matthew 5:6

> 'Let us be glad and rejoice and give Him glory, for the marriage of the Lamb has come, and His wife has made herself ready.' And to her it was granted to be arrayed in fine linen, clean and bright, for the fine linen is the righteous acts of the saints.
>
> Revelations 19:7–8

Another crucial point to understand is that Christ Himself is our righteousness. Not His righteousness, for that is forever His and what qualified Him to be ours. When the Father looks upon a believer, what He looks for is Christ Himself, as a garment, as it were, covering the nakedness of a sinner. This is a very important distinction.

But then a question arises: if He Himself is our righteousness, which has been freely given to us by faith alone, why the need to hunger and thirst for something we already have?

The answer, of course, is the same as in all things spiritual: Christ. For He is not only our righteousness on the "outside," He is also our righteousness on the inside, where He has come to dwell once we believe unto salvation. We are acceptable to God by the presence of our outer righteousness, His Son, but we will be rewarded on the basis of what we allow the Christ within to be in our lives.

Some believe that being a believer automatically qualifies one to be invited to the Marriage Supper of the Lamb. But Revelations 19:7–8 seems to indicate that the invitation is on the basis of righteous acts, which is what supplies the fine linen and makes the Bride ready to be married to Christ.

Of course, these righteous acts are also Christ Himself, but the only way for them to manifest is through death of self. In Matthew 25, the wise virgins were those who were willing to make that sacrifice, being rewarded each time by extra oil; the foolish virgins, on the other hand, were unwilling, therefore their lamps began to go out when the Bridegroom delayed His arrival. All ten were virgins; all ten belonged to the Lord. The five foolish ones will not go to hell, but neither will they attend the Marriage Supper.

The problem in this matter can come by way of ignorance as well as unwillingness. So many try to create their own righteousness by imitating Christ and walking by His teachings. Such a thing cannot be done by natural strength and merely gaining knowledge of the Way and trying to apply it. Tiring and compromise eventually set in, and all such efforts fail. Instead of living water and fresh bread, such a person settles for stale crumbs and stagnant water and never comes into the fullness of his heritage.

No righteousness exists outside Christ Himself. He, His very person, is what secures our acceptance by God, and His Life lived out through us is the righteousness that will be rewarded in the Kingdom. Anything else is filthy rags.

This righteousness is what we must continue to hunger and thirst for until He comes; for He promised that if we do, we will be filled. Not only when the Kingdom arrives, but even now as we aim for the high mark of our calling in Christ Jesus. Without these fillings, in fact, real spiritual growth will come to an end. When the time of separation comes, all those who have ceased hungering and thirsting for righteousness, or have been unwilling to pay its price, will be numbered with the foolish and miss the Marriage Supper.

The Merciful

> Blessed are the merciful, for they shall obtain mercy.
>
> Matthew 5:7

What does it mean to be merciful? What is mercy? Mercy is extending grace even when it is not deserved. Forgiveness, loving in spite of what has offended, that is mercy; the very thing God has poured out on us (and continues to pour and pour!). Matthew 7:1 and 2 says this: "Judge not, that you be not judged. For with what measure you use, it will be measured back to you."

To refrain from judgment is to show mercy. And the reward for such behavior is to receive mercy ourselves. We have already said that we will continue receiving mercy from God throughout our earthly sojourn. But another time will also come when our need for mercy will be great: at the judgment seat of Christ.

When we stand before the Lord, and we see through His eyes how often we have failed Him, falling short of the glory due His Name, we will need His mercy more than ever. And He will deal with us in one of two ways: harshly or with mercy. If we have been one who has allowed His mercy to come forth in our lives in our treatment of others, He will act most mercifully to us at that time. If, on the other hand, we have been hard on others in this life, He will be less merciful to us. He will measure back to us what we have measured out to others.

What causes us to be backbiters, judgmental and unmerciful? Self, plain and simple. We have been slighted or offended, so we respond devoid of any mercy. We did not deserve such treatment, we were unfairly or even falsely accused, we, we, we ... What did the Lord do when He was being crucified by evil men? He said: "Father, forgive them, for they do not know what they do" (Luke 23:34). He who had done no wrong, pleading for the Father to have mercy on those who were killing Him!

The Scriptures tell us that we do not wrestle against flesh and blood but against demonic forces behind the appearance of things. (Ephesians 6:12) Those who treat us unjustly have been accessed by the enemy, and Jesus exhorts us to pray for them. If we do not, but act in an unmerciful manner in response, we ourselves have also been accessed by the enemy! We must allow Christ to come out in such situations, if we are to obtain mercy ourselves.

The Pure in Heart

Blessed are the pure in heart, for they shall see God.

Matthew 5:8

Keep your heart with all diligence, for out of it spring the issues of life.

Proverbs 4:23

The lamp of the body is the eye. If therefore your eye be single (good), your whole body will be full of light.

Matthew 6:22

What resides in the heart of a man is who he is—not what he appears to be on the outside, but what is on the inside. A man may seem to be very godly, all his behavior and responses proper and righteous. But on the inside he may be a very different man. Some Pharisees were men such as these, clean outwardly but unrighteous within.

God will allow crises to come into our lives for us to see who we really are. When there is no time to prepare ourselves, when the heat of the moment is so intense that we cannot think it out first, what pours forth from our mouths and our actions is who we are. God already knows it, for He is a "discerner of the thoughts and intents of the heart" (Heb. 4:12b). But He wants us to know it.

Any impurity of heart clouds our vision of God. Clear revelations can only pass through a pure heart. So what is the path to a pure heart? Christ. Christ taking up residence and being welcomed into our whole being, spirit, soul, and body. The Spirit of Christ, who alone can show us the Father clearly. Those who have a single eye, focused on Christ alone, have a pure heart, for their whole body will be filled with light. Christ Himself is that Light, and it is by Him that anyone sees God.

The extent to which we have surrendered our lives to the Life of Christ, what is commonly called consecration, is the measure of clarity by which we see God. Holding out the smallest thing can cause a false impression of the Lord. The greater the consecration, the truer the vision of God. *Now* in the form of the revelations of the Holy Spirit; in the Kingdom, God Himself, face-to-face, seeing Him as He really is, no longer through a darkened glass. For it is in His Light that we see light.

The Peacemakers

> Blessed are the peacemakers, for they shall be called the sons of God.
>
> Matthew 5:9

> …endeavoring to keep the unity of the Spirit in the bond of peace.
>
> Ephesians 4:3

The earth has been in turmoil and tumult since the rebellion in Eden. No lasting peace has ever appeared. The heart of man is easily stirred to enmity, even as Satan's is filled with hatred toward God and righteousness. Such will be the condition on earth until Jesus comes again.

But the Father is the ultimate peacemaker, having gone to the utmost to reconcile sinful man to Himself. And His Son is the Prince of Peace, so there are now peacemakers among us, those with the heart of the Father and the Son. And it is they who shall be called the sons of God in the Kingdom.

In the Body of Christ, unity and peace already exist. We are not called to create peace but to keep it, to maintain what is already there by way of the Holy Spirit. Any discord between brothers and sisters in the Lord can be peacefully resolved if the

Holy Spirit is allowed to monitor the situation. For He is the Spirit of peace and unity, always working to bring the true Body of Christ into oneness.

It is only through the resistance of man that this effort fails. Such schisms, divisions, disputes will always prevent the blessings of God from fully manifesting; which is sadly the state of most of the church today. Those who will suffer the most loss at the judgment seat of Christ will be those who had divided the precious Body of Christ. We should, therefore, not be drawn into such skirmishes, but rather be ministers of reconciliation. For this is the will of God.

Of course, it all starts with self. So long as self is not at peace, discord is inevitable. The strife among the nations and within families and the church all start from no peace in the individual souls of men and women. One who is not at peace himself can never be a true peacemaker. And there can be no rest, as described in Hebrews 4, until a state of peace has been reached. Without peace within, restlessness is the result. Only Christ is the source of such peace.

The Blessings of Persecution

> Blessed are those who are persecuted for righteousness' sake, for theirs is the kingdom of Heaven.
>
> Matthew 5:10

> Blessed are you when they revile and persecute you, and say all kinds of evil against you falsely for My sake. Rejoice and be exceedingly glad, for great is your reward in Heaven, for so they persecuted the prophets who were before you.
>
> Matthew 5:11–12

Living the life of the Beatitudes will cause persecution and tribulation. The first seven blessings (Matthew 5:3–9) all describe the living qualities of those who will inhabit the Kingdom to rule and reign with Christ. All such lives lived now, however, are so contrary to the ways of the world and its prince that suffering will be called for.

Indeed, the Scriptures admonish us to have a mind to suffer, and assure us that all such suffering shall not be in vain. The early disciples, and many others since, counted it a privilege to share in the sufferings of Christ. The world that hates Him will also hate us if we truly follow Him.

All the blessings of the Beatitudes lead to the Kingdom of Heaven in one form or another. But only the ninth one is "greatly" rewarded, which must be so great that it should cause us not only to rejoice but to do so "exceedingly!" The details of the blessing are not given, but with Christ Himself being so emphatic about them, they must be magnificent indeed.

Jesus said that the servant is not greater than the Master, and that when they hate us, they are actually hating Him; He whom we love so much. It is this love for Him that should cause us to be willing to suffer all things for His sake.

Another Scripture assures us that only by going through much tribulation will anyone enter the Kingdom. Suffering seems, therefore, to be part of the price of admission. He paid everything for us. How can we pay less for Him? In 2 Corinthians, chapter 4, the apostle Paul encouraged us for those times when we suffer for Christ's sake:

> Therefore do not lose heart. Even though our outward man is perishing, yet the inward man is being renewed day by day. For our light affliction, which is but for a moment, is working for us a far more exceeding and eternal weight of glory.
>
> 2 Corinthians 4:16–17

Highly blessed is the servant who suffers for His Master!

BEFORE GOING ON

It seems appropriate to summarize what has been said to this point. We have stated that the eternal purpose of God is to sum up all things in His Son, so that Christ is all-in-all, everything in the universe filled with nothing but His Life and glory. That purpose has never changed and will not change; what God has ordained will indeed come to pass. But two problems arose that delayed the consummation of the Father's purpose: the rebellion of Satan and the fall of man.

The dominion the Creator had given to man to exercise as God's delegated authority upon the earth was lost. In the process, man was greatly diminished in his makeup: his spirit, that part capable of communing with God, became as though dead, and man was cast from the presence of God. Man in a very real sense became his own god, his soul (mind, will, and emotions) directing his life. The way back to a holy God seemed impossible.

Mankind wandered the earth for millennia in this condition. We touched on the high points of the history of his fallen state. Not even by choosing a people of His own and giving those people a Law to live by could God obtain that for which He was looking. Man in his natural state was beyond repair.

It remained for God alone to supply the answer to man's dilemma. So in the fullness of time, He sent His own Son, as a man born of a woman and under the Law, to redeem man and restore man's makeup and position; to quicken man's spirit back to life, and through the work of the Holy Spirit, to return the spirit to its rightful place, the instrument to commune with the living God, allowing Him to direct life. In that same process, the soul was to return to its intended purpose, a steward of the spirit.

But this can only be fully achieved by exchanging our life (even in a redeemed state) for the Life of Christ that is within us. That is the only way Christ can become "all-in-all" in our lives. Just such a Life is what the Beatitudes are all about: those who have overcome self and live by the Life of the Spirit of Christ, exhibiting the traits of Matthew 5:1–12. These are the overcomers of Revelation 2 and 3, the wise virgins of Matthew 25, the Shulamite maiden at the end of the Song of Solomon.

The Lord is looking for such men and women, for these are the sons of God spoken of in Romans 8:19, and it is these who shall usher in the Kingdom. These will have become the true and pure Body of Christ, the Bride who has made Herself ready. Until She appears and manifests Herself, Christ will delay His return.

But Peter tells us that we can "hasten" such a day!

> Therefore, since all these things will be dissolved, what manner of persons ought you to be in holy conduct and godliness, looking for and hastening the coming of the day of God?
>
> 2 Peter 3:11–12a,

We have also seen that for the full Life of Christ deposited within all believers to come forth, the death of self must occur. This is the kind of repentance John the Baptist announced as necessary, and also the message of Jesus Himself and all the early disciples. We must die so that Christ might live. No self-improvement plan will do, only total death of the old man, including even what we would call "good" things, abilities, dispositions, gifts, etc. Only that which passes through death and comes out on the other side, in resurrection, is of any use to God.

The new man, who is raised and has ascended with Christ, must surrender his life as well: to the Life of Christ within. For it is only by Him coming forth that God's eternal purpose can be achieved. Then the Father will truly be the God of both the Heavens and earth again.

So the Father's eternal purpose of giving Christ the preeminence in all things was advanced to its next stage by the coming of Jesus, who brought the Kingdom of Heaven with Him. By total obedience to the will of God, Jesus carried out the plan to achieve His Father's purpose.

That Life of absolute submission to the will of God now resides in all born-again believers, the Kingdom of Heaven within. It is the very Life and power that raised Jesus from the dead (Eph. 1:20); and which operates by a higher law, "the law of the Spirit of Life in Christ Jesus" (Rom. 8:2). This and this alone is what sets us free from the law of sin and death.

Now that we have seen both the eternal purpose of God and the plan for its success, we need to explore and understand the provisions within the plan: how it works, its dynamics, how we are to make it our own, a living reality. But before we do that, let us return to the Sermon on the Mount and the parables concerning the Kingdom of Heaven to see what other nuggets we might glean.

THREE VIEWS OF THE KINGDOM OF HEAVEN

> And in the days of these kings the God of Heaven will set up a kingdom which shall never be destroyed; and the kingdom shall not be left to other people; it shall break in pieces and consume all these kingdoms, and it shall stand forever.
>
> Daniel 2:44

> I was watching in the night visions, and behold, One like the Son of Man, coming with the clouds of Heaven! He came to the Ancient of Days, and they brought Him near before Him. Then to Him was given dominion and glory and a kingdom, that all peoples, nations, and languages should serve Him. His dominion is an everlasting dominion, which shall not pass away, and His kingdom the one which shall not be destroyed.'
>
> Daniel 7:13–14

The Kingdom of Heaven is spoken of in at least three ways in Scripture: in the Old Testament, in the Sermon on the Mount, and in the parables (Matthew 13 and 25). Distinguishing these three views will help us to not confuse the meaning of the Word in all three places.

Daniel tells us twice that the Heavens shall rule the earth. God will once again be the God of earth as well as Heaven. In establishing that Kingdom, He will fulfill two lines of promise: one, to the Jewish people, and secondly, to the born-again overcomers in Christ.

The Jewish nation of Israel has never occupied all the land promised to Abraham by God. Several places were never conquered. When the Millennial Kingdom is established, the chosen people of God will at long last live in the whole land and never be driven out again. This is the aspect of the Kingdom that the Old Testament dwells upon: what it will be like, on the inside, once it comes about, and God will have proved Himself faithful to Abraham, Isaac, and Jacob.

But the Kingdom described in the parables is seen from a different point of view: from the outside, what its outward appearance will be like. Thus, the parable of the ten virgins begins with the words: "Then the kingdom of Heaven shall be likened..." (Matthew 25:1a). This parable, as well as many others, focuses on what the Kingdom will be "like." Of course, the Kingdom here is the aspect of the Kingdom which fulfills the promise to the church: "To him who overcomes, I will grant to sit with me on my throne as I also overcame and sat down with my Father on His throne" (Revelation 3:21) ... to rule and reign with Christ.

The Sermon on the Mount, on the other hand, describes what type of people these overcomers will be. For the people of the Kingdom are the crux of the matter. Until they come forth and manifest, neither the external nor the internal qualities of the Kingdom matter; the manifestation of the sons of God is central.

The King will not have a Kingdom until He has a people. Wherever He truly has a people, even today, the Kingdom has already come for them; Jesus confirmed this when He said, "But if I cast out demons by the Spirit of God, surely the kingdom of God has come upon you" (Matthew 12:28).

So when the sons of men do these same miracles by the Spirit of God (these things and greater things than these), for them the Kingdom of Heaven is here now! And it is these who shall rule and reign with Christ in the Millennial Kingdom.

Some believers teach that all Christians will rule and reign with Christ in the Kingdom. But how can that be? The gift of salvation is freely given by faith alone. There is nothing to overcome in that; it is a gift from Christ because He overcame both sin and self.

What must be defeated to be an overcomer is self, which is not free; it in fact costs one everything. Why would the Lord make such distinctions when He judged the seven churches in Revelation 2 and 3, and only make promises of Kingdom blessings to those who overcome? Why would He warn us to "watch and pray" (for we know not when He will return) if all believers are going when He arrives?

The sad conclusion to this line of thinking is this: believers will either rule and reign with Christ during the thousand years, or they will not be there at all. The fate of the five foolish virgins is unclear. We know they will miss the Wedding Supper of the Lamb, but what will they be doing for a thousand years? Learning then what they should have learned during their lives upon the earth? These are indeed serious matters.

THE FRUIT OF THE BEATITUDES

'You are the salt of the earth; but if the salt loses its flavor, how shall it be seasoned? It is then good for nothing but to be thrown out and trampled underfoot by men. You are the light of the world. A city that is set on a hill cannot be hidden. Nor do they light a lamp and put it under a basket, but on a lamp-stand, and it gives light to all who are in the house. Let your light so shine before men, that they may see your good works and glorify your Father in Heaven.'

Matthew 5:13–16

Those believers who have the character traits of the Beatitudes will bear the marks of the Master, becoming themselves both salt and light to a dying world. How is it that this salt and light will manifest, and what will be their effects?

Salt has long been used as a preservative in many parts of the world to prevent spoilage. Certainly the world has become so corrupted that nothing can reverse the process of its decay except the return of Christ; but the life of a believer is to stop the corruption from advancing further. We do that by demonstrating and maintaining the victory of Christ on the cross, by His Life coming forth as our own. The Christian is to stand for righteousness, both in prayer and godly living until Christ returns to set all things right. Such a life is a salty one.

Salt has also long been used as a curative agent applied to draw out infection and heal wounds to the body; in like manner, the life of a Christian is to have this effect on those infected by the ravages of sin. If properly applied and received, healing takes place, the Holy Spirit doing the work.

Salt also enhances the flavor of all that is eaten. Thus our lives should give off a tasty savor to the lives around us and attract them to partake. For we have tasted the Lord and the taste is delectable, more savory than anything the world has to offer. So the very aroma of Christ should pervade the atmosphere wherever we go, whetting the appetites of those so in need of the Lord.

Salt also creates thirstiness, and our influence upon those around us should make them thirsty for what we have. This should make it much easier to lead them to the Water of Life to satisfy their thirst. And like Jesus said to the Samaritan woman at the well in John 4:14: "… but whoever drinks of the water that I shall give him will never thirst. But the water that I shall give him will become in him a fountain of water springing up into everlasting life."

But if the enemy or the cares of this world have caused us to lose our savor, how shall we ever get it back? To be sure, we will have setbacks and lulls in our progress as we walk the way of the Lord, but we should never lose our testimony; for if we do, until the Lord revives us again, we will be good for nothing.

Those whom the Lord loves He chastens, so He admonishes us in Revelation 3:2 to: "Therefore be zealous and repent." This is what we must do if we find ourselves in a place of lukewarmness toward the things of God. This is the remedy for a loss of saltiness, before all flavor is gone and we find our testimony lost and ourselves being tromped upon by the enemy, the world, and sinners. If we cannot muster the necessary zeal and repentance, remember that these too are parts of the Life within, which we can call upon to supply our need.

Jesus is the Light of the world, so when His Light within shines out through us, we too become lights to the world around us. The things in darkness are exposed by light, so our lives serve as judgment upon the evil that surrounds us. Sinful man hates the light for this very reason; our light will, therefore, either attract to the Lord those in sin, or cause them to hate us. Either way, we are to let it shine, not cover or hide it as some believers do for fear of standing out as being different.

We *are* different. We must be different. We must not be ashamed of the gospel of Christ, which is the source of our Light, but proclaim it by our very lives, so our good works will bring glory to our Father in Heaven. Salt and light are indeed fruit that is produced by those who live out the Life of Christ, described so beautifully in the Beatitudes.

A HIGHER LAW

'Do not think that I came to destroy the Law or the Prophets. I did not come to destroy but to fulfill. For assuredly, I say to you, till Heaven and earth pass away, one jot and one tittle will by no means pass from the law till all is fulfilled. Whoever therefore breaks one of the least of these commandments, and teaches men so, shall be called least in the kingdom of Heaven; but whoever does and teaches them, he shall be called great in the kingdom of Heaven. For I say to you, that unless your righteousness exceeds the righteousness of the scribes and Pharisees, you will by no means enter the kingdom of Heaven.'

Matthew 5:17–20

Matthew 5:1–16 describes the kind of people who will rule and reign with Christ in the Millennial Kingdom: those who live out, in this life, the qualities of the Beatitudes, thus overcoming self and allowing Christ to be their Life.

Next, the Lord turned our attention back to the Law and the Prophets. What did Jesus mean by this term? My conclusion is that He meant the whole Old Testament, including but not limited to the Ten Commandments and the Law of Moses. We know that by the works of the Law, no one can be justified before God. They are insufficient, and no man can keep them perfectly.

So Christ came to bring a higher "law," one that would complete the efficacy of the first, and one that man through Christ can achieve. Christ came to fill up the old, taking it to a higher level, thus replacing it by the new. And it is this new, higher law that Jesus taught on the Mount.

In the Sermon on the Mount, Jesus indeed announced the coming of that higher law, that which the apostle Paul called the law of the Spirit of Life in Christ Jesus. For any law to be overcome (and not just hindered from working) a higher law is required to be in place. And this is exactly what Christ has deposited inside every believer: His Life, which operates by the Law of the Spirit, and it is this law which sets us free from the law of sin and death, a seemingly inexorable but lower law which has been in operation since the fall in Eden. The Law and the Prophets could never overcome the law of sin and death; only the Law of Christ can.

The Old Testament era lasted from Moses to John the Baptist: "For all the prophets and the law prophesied until John" (Matthew 11:13), Jesus told us. That is why verse 11 of the same chapter says that the least in the Kingdom of Heaven is greater than John; he was still under the Law and the Prophets and therefore, though a great man, he never lived under the new law.

In verse 19 of Matthew 5, what are the "least of these commandments" referring to, the old commandments or the new? It has to be the new commandments, the teachings of Jesus on the Mount; because it is only by keeping them that anyone can even enter the Kingdom of Heaven. We know that the old commandments could never achieve that purpose.

Then the matter of the *least* and the *great* in the Kingdom was discussed in this passage: those who teach men to observe these commandments of the Mount but do not keep them themselves shall be called least in the Kingdom (but note such a person will still be in the Kingdom, and greater than John the Baptist therefore). The one who shall be called great in the Kingdom of

Heaven is he who both teaches and keeps this teaching himself. Otherwise, the Mount teaching is no more than a list of ideals which no man can live.

Next, Jesus began to compare and contrast the two laws, introducing a particular one by saying, "You have heard it was said to those of old ... but I say to you ... "

In each case, the Lord showed that the new law presents a much higher standard than that of the old. But if no man could keep the old law, how can anyone keep the new one? That is the logical question that should arise in our minds as we read the Sermon on the Mount.

And the only possible answer is, "We can't," which is a most marvelous revelation and realization. It is the key that points us to Christ. He is the only one who can keep (and has kept) such an exacting law; and it is His Life, deposited within us at the moment of salvation that must be released if we are to rise to the level of the new law and enter the Kingdom of Heaven.

Since He must be all-in-all, He must also be the very source of our victory gained through the operation of the new law. It is His Life and His Life alone that can attain to such a standard: praise His Name and His Life forever!

The Lord then addressed those who cannot enter the Kingdom of Heaven when He declared: "I say unto you, that except your righteousness shall exceed the righteousness of the scribes and Pharisees, you shall in no way enter the kingdom of Heaven" (Matthew 5:20).

The scribes and the Pharisees were under the old law, so their righteousness could never measure up to the demands of the new law taught by Jesus on the Mount. And only those who through the Life of Christ do measure up to the new law shall be a part of the coming Millennial Kingdom: it is insufficient for a believer to simply *have* the Life of Christ; that Life must truly *become* one's life.

Anyone who simply tries hard in his own power to live by the standards of the Sermon on the Mount places himself back under the old law again! It is crucial that we see this distinction; it will be the worst of tragedies to those who hear: "Assuredly, I say to you, I do not know you" (Matthew 25:12).

THE LORD'S PRAYER

'In this manner, therefore, pray: Our Father in Heaven, hallowed be your name, your kingdom come, your will be done on earth as it is in Heaven. Give us this day our daily bread. And forgive us our debts, as we forgive our debtors. And do not lead us into temptation, but deliver us from the evil one. For yours is the kingdom and the power and the glory forever.'

Matthew 5:9–13

But seek first the kingdom of God and His righteousness, and all these things shall be added to you.

Matthew 6:33

After using several commands of the old law and showing how the new law demands even more from us, and giving some examples of how the law of the Spirit of Life in Christ Jesus will manifest itself in real-life situations; and adding a few warnings, Jesus then taught the disciples how to pray; prayer that hits the mark and is most acceptable to God.

This pattern for true prayer has become known as the Lord's Prayer, and unfortunately has been repeated word-for-word over the centuries as some kind of holy mantra, when the Lord's intention was to show us the important elements of prayer that is well-pleasing to God.

Due to the fact that this teaching on prayer occurs within the context of Kingdom Life, it seems clear that this is a Kingdom prayer, to be prayed by those whose greatest desire is the coming of the Kingdom and its King. In the same chapter of Matthew (6:33), Jesus commanded us to seek the Kingdom *first*, above all other things, for once the Kingdom arrives, all the other issues of life will be settled. The eyes of Christ, the Father, and the Holy Spirit have all been on the Kingdom for a long time, so isn't that where our eyes and heart should be as well?

The prayer opens by giving the Father the homage due Him. It is an introduction of adoration and dependence. Independence and rebellion against authority is what rules the earth, the fruit of original sin. The total obedience of Jesus, even unto death, reestablished the authority of God, and He is the first-born of others like Himself, those of the Kingdom who bow to the authority of the Father in all things. Such an attitude is the key to victory!

The very first request of the prayer is for the Kingdom to come. Man tends to worry about everything else in his life, the material things, neglecting to pray for the Kingdom first. The beautiful part about making the coming of the Kingdom our chief concern, and praying for it, is that Jesus promises that all those other things which preoccupy us will be added as a bonus if we pray aright!

That is why another scripture says: "Therefore humble yourselves under the mighty hand of God, that He may exalt you in due time, casting all your care upon Him, for He cares for you" (1 Peter 5:7). We are to be anxious for nothing, seeking first the very heart of God, knowing He will take care of us. In fact, the very next verse of the Lord's Prayer assures that.

If we are to pray the Kingdom prayer until He comes, the enemy will work hard to prevent such petitions. One way is to cause us problems in the area of finances and provisions that are necessary for life. Therefore, the Lord instructed to pray: "Give us this day our daily bread" (Matthew 6:11). This is another way of telling us that if we put the Kingdom first, He will provide our daily needs. Notice there is no need to store up our necessities, but to ask the Lord for them daily. This expresses our dependence on the Lord and our faith that He will feed us the food allotted to us. (Proverbs 30:6).

However, we should never grow fat and lazy on the blessings of the Lord. He provides our needs that we might continue living the Kingdom Life and praying for the Kingdom until He comes. So often throughout Scripture, once rich blessings come upon God's people, they tend to forget their dependence on Him; this is a trap we must avoid at all costs.

Another way Satan attempts to disarm believers from true prayer is through the temptations of the flesh; he works hard to get us to sin. When we do, he brings condemnation, telling us we are no good and that God does not listen to us anymore, anything to keep us from praying the Father's heart.

But we have an advocate with the Father, even Jesus Christ the righteous, and if we confess our sins, He will forgive us and cleanse us of all unrighteousness: hence this part of the Lord's prayer, a plea to be forgiven and be made clean again, so that we can live and pray for the Kingdom.

But a condition for our forgiveness is given: we are forgiven *as* we forgive others who may have transgressed against us. This is so crucial to see. Apparently we will be forgiven only in the measure we have forgiven others. Remaining unforgiving makes this prayer a curse and not a blessing, implying that if we do not forgive others, He will not forgive us. Such a person will be stunted in his spiritual growth and be of no use to God in praying the prayer of the Kingdom.

James 5:16 says: "Confess our trespasses to one another, and pray for one another, that you may be healed. The effective, fervent prayer of a righteous man avails much." The sickness here is unforgiveness, which must be confessed and prayed over for healing to come. Once healed, the one who was sick can then pray fervently and effectually for the Kingdom and whatever else the Lord wants accomplished. But the unrighteousness of unforgiveness cannot remain if effectual prayer is to go forth.

The Lord even instructed us to ask the Father to be protected from temptation: "And do not lead us into temptation, but deliver us from the evil one."

In other words, "Do not even allow us to go there, Lord, into that area where we struggle so and might fail you. Protect us from even the temptation to fall and become ineffectual in doing and praying your will." This is indeed a great request and shield of protection, for the Lord will answer, and at times will even interrupt the circumstances the enemy has arranged for our downfall. At other times, He may allow us to go through the temptation, for us to see if we have indeed overcome a particular weakness. Either way, it is for our good that He works!

"For Yours is the kingdom and the power and the glory forever. Amen" (v. 13).

The prayer ends on the same note as it began, bowing to the authority, power, and glory of God. This perfectly frames our prayer and brings great honor to the Father, confessing that His desires are our desires, and that we truly consider His Son to be all-in-all and the sum of all things. That we pledge our lives and our prayers to the Kingdom until it comes upon the earth, even as it already has in our heart.

One last point here: Jesus was the first ever to address God as *Father*. We know that as the only begotten Son, He had every right to do so. But as the man Jesus, such a thing was unheard of, even blasphemy. The word Abba was used later, referring to God, an even more intimate way of speaking. What was Jesus teaching us by doing such a thing?

Surely the Lord was showing us that God is not some awesome but distant, detached, and impersonal power beyond the reach of man. In fact, He is as close as our own heart and more caring than we could ever imagine, with a great desire to be as intimate with us as a father is to his own child. Glory be to His Name forever and ever!

Praying in this manner from our hearts and spirits indicates that Christ has become all-in-all for us; and that the result of making Him the sum of all things, even the coming of the Kingdom of Heaven to earth, is our most fervent desire.

FURTHER TEACHINGS

> And so it was, when Jesus had ended these sayings, that the people were astonished at his teaching, for He taught them as one having authority, and not as the scribes.
>
> Matthew 7:28, 29

After teaching the disciples how to pray, Jesus continued with sayings, exhortations, and warnings, so that the kind of people who will make up the Kingdom became clearer and clearer. He taught and spoke with the authority of God, for He was the first man to enter the Kingdom of Heaven, which requires absolute obedience to the will of God.

Only He who is under authority has authority, whether it be demonstrated by words or actions. All that Jesus was as a man and is as the Christ of God is contained in this so-called Sermon on the Mount; this is the distilled version of who He is and who we are expected to be as we allow His Life to become ours. Only those who do so will enter the Kingdom of Heaven.

THE PURPOSE OF THE PARABLES

> Then He spoke many things to them in parables, saying…
>
> Matthew 13:3a

> And the disciples came and said to Him, 'Why do you speak to them in parables?' He answered and said to them, 'Because it has been given to you to know the mysteries of the kingdom of Heaven, but to them it has not been given.'
>
> Matthew 13:10–11

After He was accused by the Jews of healing by the power of Beelzebub, in essence rejecting Him and blaspheming God, Jesus turned away from the Jews as a people and turned His attention more and more toward the Gentiles. Salvation was still available to any individual Israelite who would believe in the Lord, but as a nation the Jews had refused to recognize their Messiah, thus sealing the Words of prophecy concerning their fate: it will not be until the time of the Great Tribulation that they *as a nation* will embrace the Savior.

Jesus then began to teach in parables, knowing that the understanding of the gospel of the Kingdom would only be given to those who would be part of that Kingdom, whether Jew or Gentile. For all the rest, that meaning would be a mystery and remain hidden. Parables became the means of hiding the mystery. This was the Lord's answer when asked by the disciples why He chose to teach "them" in parables; it was also fulfillment of the prophecy of Isaiah, spoken by the prophet and recorded in Isaiah 6:9–10.

The parables, as we have said before, were spoken to give the appearance of the Kingdom from the outside, how it would appear to anyone observing it from without. Jesus began with the parable of the sower, with Christ Himself as the sower of the seed of the Kingdom, which He had begun to sow with His teachings on the Mount and had continued to demonstrate by His life and the miracles, signs, and wonders that followed. This parable, as well as the others, has had many interpretations, but let us not be discouraged by this; rather let us pray that the Holy Spirit will give us the true meanings and then proceed.

The Parable of the Sower

'Therefore hear the parable of the Sower: When anyone hears the word of the kingdom, and does not understand it, then the wicked one comes and snatches away what was sown in his heart. This is he who received the seed by the wayside. But he who received the seed on stony places, this is he who hears the word and immediately receives it with joy; yet he has no root in himself, but endures only for a while. For when tribulation or persecution arises because of the word, immediately he stumbles. Now he who received seed among the thorns is he, who hears the word, and the cares of this world and the deceitfulness of riches choke the word, and he becomes unfruitful. But he who received the seed on the good ground is he who hears the word and understands it, who indeed

> bears fruit and produces: some a hundred, some sixty, some thirty.'
>
> Matthew 13:18–23

Please note that the seed the sower sowed is the Word of the Kingdom, this very Word we have been exploring, the gospel of the Kingdom. Not simply the Word or gospel of salvation, but the Word expressly intended to explain the requirements for entering the thousand-year reign of Christ. This is the Word Jesus sowed, and only one group of people heard it and produced fruit.

The other three groups heard it but were disqualified: the wicked one snatched it away from those who heard it by the wayside and did not understand it (many there be who fall into this category); the second group received it in the shallow, stony ground of their hearts, and at first embraced it, but when the hot sun of tribulation and persecution came because of the Word, their poor roots caused the Word to just dry up; the third group was composed of the rich. Their material wealth blinded them to the truth of the Word of the Kingdom (the "cares" for these are many!), and they proved to be unfruitful as well.

To bear good fruit, a field must be cleared of all stones, thorns, and weeds, anything that will impede the growth of the intended crop. Next, it has to be plowed very deeply, breaking up any clods before planting. And once the seed has been planted, there must be constant care to ensure a bumper crop: cultivation, the perfect amount of water and sunlight, the addition of some kind of soil enrichment, and finally, harvest.

The same is true for the soil of the human heart. The Holy Spirit will not neglect any of the above steps. He will chasten when needed, allow certain crises to reveal the contents of the heart, persecution and tribulation will be added by the enemy and the world, but timely and cumulative revelations will also come, supplying life-giving water, light and spirit enrichment.

The human vessel must not resist or rebel against His efforts but rather yield to Him in all things, painful though they may be to the flesh. For by so doing, such a man will become an overcomer, bearing much fruit that lasts, which will follow him into the Kingdom as his reward.

O Lord, apply these truths to our hearts and show us exactly where we are in Your great purpose for our lives!

The Parable of the Tares

> Another parable He put forth to them, saying, 'The kingdom of God is like a man who sowed good seed in his field; but while the men slept, his enemy came and sowed tares among the wheat and went his way. But when the grain had sprouted and produced a crop, then the tares also appeared. So the servants of the owner came and said to him, 'Sir, did you not sow good seed in your field? How then does it have tares?' He said to them, 'An enemy has done this.' The servants said to him, 'Do you want then to go and gather them up?' But he said, 'No, lest while you gather up the tares you also uproot the wheat with them. Let both grow together until the harvest, and at the time of harvest I will say to the reapers, 'First bundle together the tares and bind them in bundles to burn them, but gather the wheat into my barn.'
>
> Matthew 13:24–30

After teaching the parable of the sower and the kind of heart He is looking for, the Lord then taught the parable of the tares to warn us of one of the ways the evil one will attempt to prevent God's eternal purpose from manifesting. For added emphasis and correct understanding, Jesus later interpreted the parable Himself.

The field is the world, and the good seeds are the sons of the Kingdom who have been produced by the sowing of the Word of the Kingdom. But Satan also planted seeds of his own, false teachings and various heresies, which produced sons of the devil. The good and bad seeds grow side by side, and the Lord forbade His servants from attempting to separate and pull out the tares: there is the danger of destroying true sons if this were done, for the good and the bad look so much alike. Instead, the angels will do the work of separation at the end of the age, bundling the tares to be burned and gathering the wheat to be taken to the barn of the Lord (the Kingdom, of course).

This parable describes exactly what has happened during the history of the church: many, some knowingly and others unwittingly, have been used by the deceptions of the enemy to stall the coming of the Kingdom and prolong Satan's reign as the prince of this world.

Apparently, there are certain varieties of tares that resemble wheat so closely that the two are almost indistinguishable. It is only when both have ripened to maturity that a distinct difference appears: the heads of the wheat are a bright golden color, but the heads of the tares are black! How easy will it be then to know one from the other, but how difficult now! That is why we are warned by John to "test the spirits whether they are of God; because many false prophets have gone out into the world…" (1 John 4:1).

Such caution will become more and more important as the end of the age approaches, for we are told that the anti-christ and the false prophet will perform many signs and wonders at that time, deceiving even the saints, "were that possible." (Praise God for those last three words!)

One of Satan's chief delights is to counterfeit the works of God, to fool those who are gullible enough to worship him in the place of the Almighty. He too is able to perform certain supernatural feats; for example, the magicians of Pharaoh in the days of Moses.

But we should never follow something just because it appears to be God. Some believers today are so hungry for signs and wonders that they seem ready to go after almost anything out of the ordinary; but we are assured by Jesus that His true sheep know His voice and will not follow another (John 10:4–5).

We must therefore stay so close to the Lord that we cannot be led astray; or as one man of God has so aptly said, we must come to know the Authentic so well that when a counterfeit looms on the horizon, we will recognize it immediately.

The Parable of the Mustard Seed

> Another parable He put forth, saying: "The kingdom of Heaven is like a mustard seed, which a man took and sowed in his field, which indeed is the least of all seeds; but when it is grown it is greater than the herbs and becomes a tree, so that the birds of the air come and nest in its branches."
>
> Matthew 13:31–32

Beginning with this parable, the Lord left us on our own; for correct understanding of this and all the remaining parables, we must rely on the revelation of the Holy Spirit. But He has been sent to teach us all truth, so His guidance is absolutely dependable!

Many have been the interpretations of this parable, most of them positive in nature: that the gospel would give rise to a magnificent church, providing a perfect place for believers to abide while waiting upon the return of the Lord. I find something wrong with this interpretation. Following as it does on the heels of the warning concerning tares, it seems to me to be an additional word of caution.

In the first two parables of Matthew 13, Jesus told us straight out concerning His sowing the Word of the Kingdom into the earth and its consequences: first of all, that only a minority of hearts would receive it and produce fruit, and secondly, that the enemy would plant all kinds of deception to give rise to his own sons, thereby withstanding the coming of the Kingdom.

In the parable of the mustard seed, He began to show us the outworking of these two dynamics, what would come forth as a result of the two plantings. This is the first parable that Jesus introduced by saying: "The kingdom is like..."

In this case, it is like a mustard seed that a man planted. The man is the Lord and the mustard seed is the Word of the Kingdom. A mustard seed is a tiny seed, therefore it is used to denote smallness, which is indeed what the Kingdom of Heaven is to the world. But something quite strange and unnatural occurred after this planting: instead of producing a small shrub, a tree came forth!

The church, which has no real connection to the ways of the world, has somehow buried deep roots into the earth and drawn from its sustenance rather than the nourishment from Heaven. And because it has become more and more like the world, the birds of the air (a definite reference to Satan) have come to nest in it.

What a tragedy! Satan saw that trying to destroy the church by force and violence was not enough, so he decided to join the church as well, and corrupt from within as well as from without!

The history of the church bears witness to this fact. The seven churches in Revelation 2 and 3 followed this very path. The first step downward occurred in Ephesus, the leaving of the "first love." Next came the intense persecution at Smyrna. At Pergamos, the first mention is made of false teaching creeping in. By the time of Thyatira, Satan himself, in the form of Jezebel, had joined and begun to take control.

At Sardis, a slight revival of some sort took place, but was superficial in nature, because the Lord said: "I know your works, that you have a name that you are alive, but you are dead. Be watchful, and strengthen the things which remain…" (Revelation 3:1b-2a).

It is not until we get to Philadelphia that we see a picture of the true church: they were small, not very strong, but they had kept His Word and not denied His Name. For those reasons and their perseverance, He promised to keep them from "… the hour of trial which shall come upon the whole world, to test those who dwell on the earth" (Revelation 3:10).

But by the time we come to Laodicea, the church had once again slipped into decline. They had become rich, certainly materially, and they also fancied, spiritually; but the Lord condemned them soundly with harsh words of warning:

> I know your works, that you are lukewarm, and neither cold nor hot. I could wish you were cold or hot. So then, because you are lukewarm, and neither cold nor hot, I will vomit you out of My mouth. Because you say, 'I am rich, have become wealthy, and have need of nothing'—and do not know that you are wretched, miserable, poor, blind, and naked—'I counsel you to buy from Me, gold refined in the fire, that you may be rich; and white garments, that you may be clothed, that the shame of your nakedness may not be revealed; and anoint your eyes with eye salve, that you may see. As many as I love, I rebuke and chasten. Therefore be zealous and repent.
>
> Revelation 3:15–19

Laodicea is precisely where a large part of the church is today: so much emphasis on size and splendor; the building of magnificent cathedral-type buildings and ministries; the need for more and more money; and yet, only "a form of godliness, but denying its power" (2 Timothy 3:5).

The ways of the world have certainly invaded the church, but then the Lord warned us this would happen in His teaching on the parable of the mustard seed. We must avoid such practices at all costs, or we will not have kept the Word of His patience and will have in fact denied the very things for which His Name stands.

The Parable of the Leaven

> Another parable He spoke to them: 'The kingdom of Heaven is like leaven, which a woman took and hid in three measures of meal till it was all leavened.'
>
> Matthew 13:33

This parable is another warning concerning the future of the church. Something would corrupt it from within. Leaven is almost always used in a negative sense in Scripture, as it is in Matthew 16:12: "Then they understood that He did not tell them to beware of the leaven of bread, but of the doctrine of the Pharisees and Sadducees." So here and in other places, we come to see that leaven is used as a symbol of sin, false doctrine or teaching, which can only lead to one thing... *some other gospel* and the sinful behavior associated with it. Once Satan found his way into the church, false teaching was inevitable; anything that would reduce, even eliminate the power of the true gospel.

The woman here, rather than being a picture of the true church, is a female more closely related to the Jezebel of Revelation 2:20, one who claimed to be a prophetess but was actually an agent of the devil. She mixed her false teaching and salacious behavior into three measures of meal or flour, the amount normally used to bake a loaf of bread. The loaf of bread is indeed symbolic of Christ as the Bread of Life, so in sum, there would be a mixing of the false with the true, which would have the effect of corrupting the whole loaf.

But since some have remained undefiled, there being a remnant of overcomers in every age of the church, this parable seems to be pointing at some kind of large religious organization, full of pomp and splendor, but filled with deadly heresies on the inside. Several such organizations come to mind, but instead of pointing fingers at anyone, let us be careful indeed:

> Come out from among them and be separate, says the Lord. Do not touch what is unclean, and I will receive you. I will be a Father to you, and you shall be my sons and daughters, says the Lord Almighty.
>
> 2 Corinthians 6:17–18 and 2 Samuel 7:14

We must content ourselves with being like what some have called the faithful little flock, the church at Philadelphia.

The Parable of the Hidden Treasure

> "Again, the kingdom of Heaven is like treasure hidden in a field, which a man found and hid; and for joy over it he goes and sells all that he has and buys that field."
>
> Matthew 13:44

Previously, Jesus told of His sowing the Word of the Kingdom in the world and the results of its reception in the hearts of men. Additionally, in the parable of the tares, He warned us of the planting of the sons of the evil one who have also sprung up in the same field, the distortion of the true gospel by their deceptions, and of their fate.

Then in the parables of the mustard seed and leaven, He spoke of the tragic intrusion of the world and false teaching into the church, the workings of the tares. The next two parables in this series are positive ones, even triumphant and joyous, for in them the Lord spoke of the glory and the beauty He finds in the true church.

Treasure in the Scriptures often represents glory. The glory of the Davidic Kingdom was in its treasures. (1 Chronicles 27:25) And when the queen of Sheba visited Israel in the days of King Solomon, she was amazed at what she found, both in terms of his wisdom and the glory of his Kingdom. She paid homage to him by adding to his glory:

> And she gave the king one hundred and twenty talents of gold, spices in great abundance, and precious stones; there never were any spices such as those the queen of Sheba gave to King Solomon.
>
> 2 Chronicles 9:9

Then we are told of all the extravagant treasures that came to Solomon yearly. Indeed, the kingdom of Solomon serves as a type and shadow of the coming Kingdom of Christ. David had defeated all the enemies of Israel, even as our Lord will have done before His return, making way for the glory of His Kingdom.

The man in this parable is surely Jesus, who found the glory of the Kingdom to come, but then due to His rejection, hid it again. For it would not be His until He paid a great price for it, selling all that He had (His very life) that He could return and claim it. The joy of such a discovery was so great that nothing was too big a price to pay, for the glory that shall be revealed in that day will be more than words can express; Jesus saw it then, and we shall be part of it in the Kingdom.

Hallelujah!

The Parable of the Pearl

> "Again, the kingdom of Heaven is like a merchant seeking beautiful pearls, who when he had found one pearl of great price, went and sold all that he had and bought it"
>
> (Matthew 13:45–46)

Pearls are things of beauty, used to adorn. They are created in oysters by the introduction of a foreign substance into the tender parts of the creature, that material becoming the "seed" of the pearl to come. It is most likely a painful process for the sea animal, but a thing of great beauty is produced by its suffering.

The merchant in this parable is Christ, who looks everywhere for the ones who will allow Him to do a complete work in them, those who will suffer loss for His Name's sake, loss of goods, reputation, even self. In the Song of Solomon, there are other followers after the Lord, the daughters of Jerusalem, but only one Shulamite; she is indeed a pearl of great price.

Of course Christ is searching for a whole Body of believers of such pearls, and eventually He will have them, for all things shall be summed up in Him. But for the time being, He is only able to find a few here and there. The Word assures us in many places that He will have the delight of His heart, the prize for which He travailed. One of my favorite verses on this subject is Psalms 110:3: "Your people shall be volunteers in the day of Your power; in the beauties of holiness, from the womb of the morning, You have the dew of Your youth."

In another translation, paraphrased, this verse says that in the day of His battle, He will have His people of a willing heart; His youth will come to Him like the dew.

This is a clear reference to the chariots of Amminadab in Song of Solomon 6:12, or in the New King James, the "chariots of my noble people." The Shulamite was carried away in a vision and saw that she was not alone; many chariots were joining the battle. These are the pearls of great price the Lord is seeking.

What is a willing heart? One that will allow the Life of Christ within to do its work no matter what. The demands of that work are great, and the flesh tends to recoil, even as the oyster must when the irritating seed is planted inside it. But the willing heart has been given a vision of the Kingdom and the beauty of the King; once this happens, nothing else in the world will satisfy the heart. It cries out, "My Beloved, I must have Him!"

Nothing then is too much to give up for Him. Christ foresaw this moment, when His whole church, His Bride, was ready and arrayed in fine linen, and the eternal purpose of God was accomplished, and for that "sold all He had," even His very life. This vision gave Jesus intense joy, and gave Him the strength and courage to endure every hardship and obstacle in the way, even His death on the cross (He.12:2).

We must now endure our cross, picking it up daily for that same joy that is waiting; for when we do, we will be one of those pearls of great price with which our Lord can adorn Himself.

What joy, what a privilege!

The Parable of the Dragnet

> Again, the kingdom of Heaven is like a dragnet that was cast into the sea and gathered some of every kind, which, when it was full, they drew to shore; and they sat down and gathered the good into vessels, but threw the bad away.
>
> Matthew 13:47–48

The time of judgment has arrived in this parable. In the parables of the sower and the tares, the beginning of the Word of the Kingdom was shown, and now in the parable of the dragnet, the ending has come. This surely must be during the time of the Great Tribulation, when a mighty angel will proclaim the eternal gospel one last time to the inhabitants of the earth:

> Then I saw another angel flying in the midst of Heaven having the everlasting gospel to preach to those who dwell on the earth—to every nation, tribe, tongue, and people—saying with a loud voice, 'Fear God and give glory to Him, for the hour of His judgment has come; and worship Him who made Heaven and earth, the sea and springs of water.'
>
> Revelation 14:6–7

Although judgment will be about to fall, the mercy of God will be extended one more time to gather those who are His from the nations. So the net is this gospel of the Kingdom, which the angel will proclaim, and with it, he and other angels will draw in their catch, both believers and unbelievers. On the shore, they will sit down and separate the fish, placing the believing into a vessel for the Lord, but throwing the unbelieving away. The "good" will take their parts in the Kingdom, the "bad" destined for the lake of fire and everlasting torment.

This parable bears a resemblance to the ending of the parable of the tares and the parable of the sheep and goats in Matthew 25:31–36. Judgment will have come in all three instances: in the parable of the tares, angels will come to separate the sons of the Kingdom from the sons of Satan; in the parable of the sheep and goats, there will be a separation on the basis of how the believing Jews and other Christians are treated during the time of the Great Tribulation. The judgment of individuals is involved in the first two, but the judgment of nations in the parable of the sheep and goats.

In this group of seven parables, the Lord foretold all the events regarding the coming of the Kingdom of Heaven from beginning to end: the sowing of it into four types of hearts; what the enemy would do in response to it; how it would become corrupted by men; how Christ will eventually get what He and the Kingdom came for; and finally, the judgment of all those who refuse to receive its message.

The Lord wanted to make sure the disciples understood all He had taught, so He asked them and they answered, "Yes, Lord," in verse 51. Then in verse 52, Jesus concluded this section of His teaching with these words: "Therefore every scribe instructed concerning the Kingdom of Heaven is like a householder who brings out of his treasure things new and old."

By this He meant that everybody who hears and understands the gospel of the Kingdom, even as the disciples had, will be able to see the connection between the Old Testament and the New, both of them the source of great treasure, even Christ Himself!

There are many treasures in such an understanding, but the choicest is identifying the eternal purpose of God, and the plan the Father, Son, and Holy Spirit have used to accomplish that purpose: the coming of Christ from the Kingdom of God, bringing with Him the Kingdom of Heaven, and through His perfect life and sacrificial death, planting that Kingdom in the heart and spirit of every born-again believer.

This indeed is our heritage. In Part Three we will see how to claim and live it... now, in *this* life! In the parables that follow, Jesus gives warnings and the need for watchfulness. He does not wish for any to miss the Kingdom. In some cases, He warns those on the outside, sinners who refuse to come to Him at all. In other parables, He admonishes watchfulness for those who do believe but have not come to the place of total surrender to Him. In the case of unbelievers, hellfire awaits. For believers who remain carnal and serve God from their souls rather than their spirits, He makes it quite clear that they will miss the Marriage Supper of the Lamb and will not rule and reign with Him in the Kingdom.

PARABLES OF WATCHFULNESS

The Parable of the Fig Tree

> Now learn this parable of the fig tree: when its branch has already become tender and put forth leaves, you know that summer is near. So you also, when you see all these things, know that it is near—at the doors! Assuredly, I say to you, this generation will be no means pass away till all these things take place.
>
> Matthew 24:32–34

To better understand what Jesus spoke here concerning the fig tree, we must return to Matthew 21:18–19: "Now in the morning, as He returned to the city, He was hungry. And seeing a fig tree by the road, He came to it, and found nothing on it but leaves, and said to it, 'Let no fruit grow on you ever again.' Immediately the fig tree withered away."

In the Scriptures, the fig tree is often used as a symbol for Israel and the Jews. So when Jesus found no fruit on the tree, even though it was time for it to bear, He cursed it, and it immediately withered. The leaves on the tree were supposed to be an indicator of fruit, but there was none: likewise, the Jews, living under the Law, were all outward show but with no evidence of life. By cursing the tree, Christ was actually condemning the Jews living under the Law: such a life could never produce the fruit of righteousness.

But in verse 32 of Matthew 24, Jesus spoke of the fig tree beginning to show forth life (the branches becoming tender and putting forth leaves). This is surely a sign to the church, for when at least a remnant of Jewish people begin to turn to Christ as their Messiah, we can know the end is near. Only by turning away from the old law and receiving Christ as their Savior can any Jew bear real fruit that lasts. So we can see from all this that Matthew 24:1–31 is mainly speaking to the Jews, and that verses 31–46 are addressed to the church.

The Jews as a nation are still in winter and a time of tribulation, and this will persist until spring arrives (tender branches with leaf buds); then, just as surely as summer follows spring, many Jews will come to Christ and enter the Millennial Kingdom to receive all the promises of God given to Abraham, Isaac and Jacob.

Even today, in our time, more Jews are becoming believers in Christ than at any other time in history; the church should be aroused and note this with joy and a sense of anticipation. Surely the Kingdom is not far off! As never before, we must pray for God's chosen people, that those who are His might be drawn to their Savior.

Israel became a sovereign nation once again in 1948. Based on that fact, some predicted that by 1988, the rapture would occur. But that interpretation was erroneous for many different reasons. First of all, Jesus clearly stated in verse 36 that in spite of all parts of His answer concerning end-times, no one would know exactly when it will take place. Men have nevertheless repeatedly made such predictions. The Seventh Day Adventists predicted 1844 would be the year of Christ's return. The Watchtower Society chose the year 1900. Any and all such dates will fail.

The 1988 predictions were made by adding forty years (commonly thought of as a "generation" in the Western world) to 1948, the year Israel became a nation once again. But of course, 1988 has come and gone, and Christ has still not returned. This confusion as well as others, I believe, rests upon a correct understanding of verse 34: "Assuredly, I say unto you, this generation will by no means pass away till all these things take place."

This verse certainly does raise problems. What did the Lord mean by "this generation?" Did He mean the generation of the disciples in a literal sense? Many skeptics have used this argument to discredit Christ and Christianity; for such an understanding would be proof that either Jesus was in error, or that the prophecy has already come to pass, some citing Titus's destruction of Jerusalem forty years after the Lord spoke these words.

Others have said "this generation" refers to the generation who will be alive when "all these things" (mentioned by Christ in answer to the disciples' questions of Matt. 24:3) begin to happen; that generation will not pass away till the events of Christ's prophecy come to pass.

The explanation of the skeptics cannot be true, and the second understanding seems a stretch. What then, did Jesus mean?

The original word for "generation" as used in this passage is "genea" which can be used in a literal, physical sense. But it can also be used in a moral sense as well, not meaning a specific period of time, such as thirty or forty years, but a period in which certain moral conditions exist. Such a "generation" continues for as long as the moral situation continues.

For example, in the Old Testament, in Deuteronomy 32:20, we read, "For they are a perverse generation, children in whom is no faithfulness." The Hebrew people had become morally degraded, perverse and faithless, for far longer than thirty or forty years, and such a "generation" would continue to exist until such corruption ended, however long that might be.

Likewise, in the New Testament, in this very book, Matthew, it says: "An evil and adulterous generation seeketh after a sign; and there shall be no sign given to it but the sign of Jonah the prophet… the men in Nineveh shall stand up in judgment of this generation, and shall condemn it" (12:39, 41a).

Such a generation would last for as long as evil and adultery prevailed, not simply from one physical generation to the next. Likewise, the moral conditions Jesus found in Israel (and indeed in the entire world) at the time of His prophecy will continue and not pass away until "after all these things come to pass." In other words, we are still part of that "generation." When all the things come to pass that Jesus prophesied, then that generation of moral degradation will end; for then Christ will return to rule and reign in righteousness. This seems the most likely interpretation of verse 34.

As in the Days of Noah

> But of that day and hour no one knows, not even the angels of Heaven, but My Father only. But as the days of Noah were, so also will the coming of the Son of Man be. For as in the days before the flood, they were eating and drinking, marrying and giving in marriage, until the day that Noah entered the ark, and did not know until the flood came and took them all away, so also will the coming of the Son of Man be. Then two men will be in the field: one will be taken and the other left. Two women will be grinding at the mill: one will be taken and the other left. Watch therefore, for you do not know what hour your Lord is coming.
>
> Matthew 24:36–42

Jesus continued His teachings on watchfulness by comparing the time of His Second Coming to the days of Noah just prior to the Great Flood. There is much to consider here.

First of all, evil abounded in the days of Noah, to the point that: "Then the Lord saw that the wickedness of man was great in the earth, and that every intent of the thoughts of his heart was only evil continually" (Genesis 6:5). Such a frightful state of affairs, but exactly the way things are rapidly becoming in the world today. Atrocities are so commonplace that people have become desensitized to them. Great complacency and apostasy have found their way into the church, with no widespread and ardent repentance to be found. Business just goes on as usual.

That is the main point in the comparison of Noah's day to our own: no one seems to notice or care so long as it does not touch their lives and disturb their merrymaking; so long as they can continue eating and drinking, marrying and giving in marriage, etc., all will be well. The pursuit of sheer pleasure and sumptuous living, with no regard for the sin that may be part of such indulgences has become epidemic in our country.

And the church of the living God has not been exempted: believers have gladly followed suit. Many churches today, some quite large, have the word "Ichabod" written above the doorway and do not even know it! For the ways of the world have become the ways of such churches, and the glory of the Lord has departed.

Judgment was closing in then, even as it is today, and when it finally does fall, the masses will be taken by complete surprise, even as the multitudes were in the days of Noah. To drive this point of readiness and watchfulness even deeper, the Lord spoke of rapture.

This controversial subject will be discussed at length in a later section, but since it is mentioned in this passage, we dare not pass it by. Two men are in the field, one taken, the other left behind; two women are at the mill, and again one is taken, the second one left.

In the days of Noah, the righteous were left behind, the unrighteous taken away by the flood. In this "parable," the righteous are taken and the unrighteous left behind. Opposites, and an argument many have used to refute the fact of rapture. But in the case of Noah, the righteous were left behind so God could start all over with man and his eternal purpose; without righteous survivors of the flood, such an endeavor would have been impossible.

In the case of rapture, a new Kingdom is in view, even the Kingdom of Heaven, and those taken from the earth prior to the Tribulation will be the first-fruits of that Kingdom. This kingdom, the kingdom of darkness, is passing away, with a new one coming; one in which Christ will at last become the sum of all things. Those who are raptured will be the very ones who have walked the way of the cross and lived out the Beatitudes, Christ being their all-in-all. They are the overcomers of Revelation, chapters 2 and 3. But the main point Jesus was making in the days of Noah comparison was this: don't be the one who is left behind!

The Parable of the Master of the House

> Watch therefore, for you do not know what hour your Lord is coming. But know this, that if the master of the house had known what hour the thief would come, he would have watched and not allowed his house to be broken into.
>
> Matthew 24:43–44

This is a parable of watchfulness. Chapter 24 of Matthew begins with the Lord telling the disciples: "Do you not see all these things? Assuredly, I say to you, not one stone shall be left here upon another, that shall not be thrown down" (verse 2). Jesus was referring to the coming destruction of the temple, and the disciples were curious as to the timing of such a tragedy and end-time events, so they asked the Lord: "Tell us, when these things will be. And what will be the sign of your coming, and of the end of the age" (verse 3b).

Jesus then answered all three questions in the remainder of chapter 24 and all of Matthew 25. He warned of the deceptions by the enemy as the end approaches, the spirit of lawlessness abounding, the coming of false prophets, wars and rumors of war, natural disasters, and signs in the Heavens—times of extreme calamities—but all of these will be but the "beginning of sorrows" (verse 8).

It is not until the gospel of the Kingdom will have been preached to all nations that the end will come (verse 14). Apparently, then, this gospel will not have been preached to all the world until the Tribulation is well underway. Many believe it will be the believing Jews who will be proclaiming it then. But that does not relieve us, as Christians, of the responsibility of preaching it now.

After warning of all the above conditions, and telling His disciples that no one knows the exact timing of them ("But of that day and hour no one knows, not even the angels of Heaven, but My Father only."—verse 36), Jesus said: "Watch therefore..." (verse 42a).

In other words, take heed, be on the alert, knowing it could happen when you least expect it. And with those words of caution, He taught the parable of the master of the house.

The house stands for the works of the believer, so the master of the house is the believer himself. The thief is the Lord, but instead of taking things away, He will come to bring greater blessings. Thieves do not warn victims that they are coming, but the Lord warned us again and again that He is coming, to be ready and watchful. In fact, the entire point of this parable and others that follow is watchfulness and the unpredictability of the Lord's return.

But 1 Thessalonians 5:4–10 assures us that we should not be taken by surprise when the Lord comes:

> But you, brethren, are not in darkness, so that this Day should overtake you as a thief. You are all sons of light

and sons of the day. We are not of the night nor of darkness. Therefore let us not sleep, as others do, but let us watch and be sober. For those who sleep, sleep at night, and those who get drunk are drunk at night. But let us who are of the day be sober, putting on the breastplate of faith and love, and as a helmet the hope of salvation. For God did not appoint us to wrath, but to obtain salvation through our Lord Jesus Christ, who died for us, that whether we wake or sleep, we should live together with Him.

1 Thessalonians 5:4–10

So the Lord has both warned and amply supplied the ability to respond wisely to the Word of His coming. All who will be taken by surprise will stand without excuse.

The Parable of the Two Servants

Therefore you also be ready, for the Son of Man is coming at an hour you do not expect. Who then is a faithful and wise servant whom his master made ruler over his household, to give them food in due season? Blessed is that servant whom his master, when he comes, will find so doing. Assuredly I say to you that he will make him ruler over all his goods. But if that evil servant says in his heart, 'My master is delaying his coming,' and begins to beat his fellow servants, and to eat and drink with the drunkards, the master of that servant will come on a day when he is not looking for him and at an hour that he is not aware of, and cut him in two and appoint him his portion with the hypocrites. There shall be weeping and gnashing of teeth.

Matthew 24:44–51

This parable and the one which follows (The Ten Virgins) both speak of reactions to the delay of the Lord and the setting up of the Kingdom. In the parable of the two servants, the evil servant counts on just such a delay, or grows weary waiting, and falls back into sin. But in the parable of the ten virgins, the foolish ones do not make provision for such a long delay, apparently thinking He will return sooner than He does. In both cases, however, it is the matter of the timing of the return that causes problems.

In this parable, the household is a picture of the church, being corporate in nature, for it speaks of "fellow servants." The servants in question have been given authority over the running of the household. One proves to be faithful and wise, while the other becomes unfaithful and foolish.

The first feeds those in the household the food they need in due season: this could be in teaching the Words the Spirit gives, encouragement to the downcast, etc.; actually, listening to the Lord and serving in whatever capacity that edifies and uplifts fellow believers and exalts the Name of the Lord. The reward for such a servant will be to be made ruler over a much greater domain in the Kingdom.

But the evil servant is one who grows tired waiting, thinking perhaps the Lord will never return, or at least not for a very long time; which will give him plenty of time to put his house back in order later. So he begins "beating" fellow servants and going the way of the worldly. Beating as used here is to misuse the authority the master has given him, lording it over them, becoming a tyrant instead of speaking the truth in love. And getting drunk with the drunkards is a blatant breach of our calling to be sanctified and separate from the world.

Such a servant will be shocked by the sudden return of his master. And his master will deal with him most harshly: he will put the servant out of the household and his presence, even as Paul advised the believers in Corinth to expel from their church the brother who was guilty of incest.

But I do not believe that the separation is to be permanent in such cases. The expulsion is for the sinner to find repentance and return to the fold, even as in the case at Corinth; for in his second letter to the Corinthians, Paul advised the church to take the guilty but repentant one back in love. But I am sure that all such believers do experience deep regret and wrenching sorrow for their actions while separated from the Body, hence the "weeping and gnashing of teeth" (verse 51b).

The Parable of the Ten Virgins

> Then the kingdom of Heaven shall be likened to ten virgins who took their lamps and went out to meet the bridegroom. Now five of them were wise, and five were foolish. Those who were foolish took their lamps and took no oil with them, but the wise took oil in their vessels with their lamps. But while the bridegroom was delayed, they all slumbered and slept. And at midnight a cry was heard: 'Behold, the bridegroom is coming; go out to meet him!' Then all those virgins arose and trimmed their lamps. And the foolish said to the wise, 'Give us some of your oil, for our lamps are going out.' But the wise answered, saying, 'No, lest there should not be enough for us and you; but go rather to those who sell, and buy for yourselves.' And while they went to buy, the bridegroom came, and those who were ready went in with him to the wedding, and the door was shut. Afterward the other virgins came also, saying, 'Lord, Lord, open to us!' But he answered and said, 'Assuredly, I say to you, I do not know you.' Watch therefore, for you know neither the day nor the hour in which the Son of Man is coming.
>
> Matthew 25:1–13

This parable, like the previous two, is one of warning and watchfulness. In this case, during the Lord's delayed return, five virgins had been watchful and doing the Lord's will and five had been foolish and had not done all they had been called to do. First of all, we must note that all ten were virgins, belonging to the Lord, so any question of the five foolish ones going to hell must be dismissed at the very outset.

All the saved are given new Life, signified by the lit lamps, but no one is given extra oil: this must be earned by walking the way of the cross, giving up self in favor of the Life of Christ within and the Kingdom of Heaven. Five had been willing to do that and five had not. And the Word says that the lamps of the foolish were "going out," not "had gone out." So the only difference between the two groups is willingness or unwillingness to surrender self. And if the Lord had not delayed His return, the foolish would have been prepared to go out to meet Him, too, along with their wiser sisters.

So in both this parable and the previous two, the delay of the Lord is what has caused the problem: in the parable of the master of the house, the believer was not ready for the Lord's return and so lost a great blessing; in the parable of the two servants, the evil servant actually began actively sinning during the delay; but the foolish virgins had simply been unwilling to sacrifice self as the Lord taught in the Beatitudes, a requirement if one is to receive the reward of the Kingdom of Heaven.

There is also the matter of sleeping to be discussed. When speaking of believers, the Word often uses the word "sleep" to mean death. So if that be true, all ten virgins had fallen asleep in the Lord and arose at His coming. But others have suggested that they were only resting, as in our need for real sleep. If that is what the Lord meant, then five had gone to bed at ease and well prepared for the Lord's return, and five had retired ill-prepared. In either case, the matter of readiness and the unpredictability of the timing of the Lord's return are the main issues.

Of course, there was no way the five wise virgins could share some of their oil with the foolish ones. The best they could do was advise them how to get it. But the hour was too late for new oil to avail; the bridegroom had come, and the time of the wedding had arrived. When the foolish virgins returned (with oil?), they were turned away by the bridegroom himself, with the words, "I do not know you" (25:12b).

This is perhaps why some have thought one of two things: that the foolish virgins had not experienced true salvation in the first place; or that they were saved but had indeed lost their state of salvation. Neither conclusion is correct: as we have already pointed out, all ten were virgins, evidence that all ten belonged to the Lord, and therefore were among the elect.

And the age-old controversy of the eternal security of the believer versus the possibility of losing salvation even after true conversion rests on an understanding of the Lord's denial of "knowing" the foolish virgins. On the surface, this appears to be saying that the foolish virgins were never saved at all; or that they had indeed been saved but had lost their salvation, hence the Lord no longer knew them. But a closer look at the word "know" helps to clear this up.

Two different words in the Greek are used to mean to "know": ginosko and oida. The word used in this passage is oida, which means knowing in a deep way, intimately, therefore to applaud or endorse. Ginosko, on the other hand, means to know in a much more objective way, as in, "I don't know the man," meaning I have never met him; I don't even know who he is.

So, the bridegroom was not saying he did not know (ginosko) the foolish virgins, for he certainly did know them in that sense. Instead, he was saying he did not know (oida) them in a way that would allow them entrance into the Wedding Supper. They indeed were the Lord's, but by name only; they were not closely enough related in their makeup (too much of self left) to be a part of the Bride, who is without stain, blot, or blemish of any kind. And of course, the foolish were not those who had been saved but had lost their salvation due to their foolishness, for salvation is not based on works but on grace alone.

As to the fate of the foolish virgins after they were denied entrance into the Wedding, we are not told. All we know for sure is that they were not part of the Bride of Christ. If hell is not their destination, then they must be going to a place where they will learn the lessons of submission and obedience that they should have learned during their days on the earth. Just how long those lessons will take to learn, again, we are not told. But what we are told is this:

"Watch therefore, for you know neither the day nor the hour the Son of man is coming" (25:13).

Let us therefore be wise while there is yet time, be watchful and be about our Father's business.

The Parable of the Talents

> For the Kingdom of Heaven is like a man traveling to a far country, who called his own servants and delivered his goods to them. And to one he gave five talents, to another two, and to another one, to each according to his own ability; and immediately he went on a journey. Then he who had received five talents went and traded with them, and made another five talents. And likewise he who had received two gained two more also. But he who had received one went and dug in the ground, and hid his lord's money. After a long time the lord of those servants came and settled accounts with them. So he who had received five talents came and brought five other talents saying, 'Lord, you delivered to me five talents; look, I have gained five more talents besides them.' His lord said to him, 'Well done, good and faithful servant; you were faithful over a few things, I will make you ruler over many things. Enter into the joy of your lord.' He also who had received two talents

came and said, 'Lord, you delivered to me two talents; look, I have gained two more talents besides them.' His lord said to him, 'Well done, good and faithful servant; you have been faithful over a few things, I will make you ruler over many things. Enter into the joy of your lord.' Then he who had received the one talent came and said, 'Lord, I knew you to be a hard man, reaping where you have not sown, and gathering where you have not scattered seed. And I was afraid and went and hid your talent in the ground. Look, there you have what is yours.' But His lord answered and said to him, 'You wicked and lazy servant, you knew that I reap where I have not sown, and gather where I have not scattered seed. So you ought to have deposited my money with the bankers, and at my coming I would have received back my own with interest. Therefore take the talent from him, and give it to him who has ten talents. For to everyone who has, more will be given, and he will have abundance; but from him who does not have, even what he has will be taken away. And cast the unprofitable servant into the outer darkness. There will be weeping and gnashing of teeth.'

Matthew 25:14–30

This parable is somewhat similar to the parable of the ten virgins, but with a key difference: in the parable of the virgins, the issue is whether one is filled with the Holy Spirit (oil) through denial of self and allowing the cross to work its way through all aspects of our lives. In this parable, the Lord deals with the use of the gifts of the Holy Spirit, something all believers receive, some receiving more and some less, according to the sovereignty of the Lord; but no one who belongs to the Lord is left with no gift whatsoever. The issue in the parable of the talents is faithfulness or unfaithfulness regarding the gifts one receives from the Lord.

 The Lord gave one servant five talents (gifts), a second two, and to a third servant He gave one. He then went into a far country; indeed this is a picture of the Lord's ascension into Heaven over two thousand years ago. He wanted to test his servants during his absence; many servants do well if their master is about, but what will they do when he is gone? This is a true test of their faithfulness. How will each use His gifts when He is not around to watch?

The servant who received five talents used them well and doubled the number he started with; likewise the second servant, who increased his talents from two to four. How is it that we can increase our gifts? By employing them well, by listening to the promptings of the Holy Spirit and taking advantage of the opportunities He presents to bring glory to the King and His Kingdom. As we faithfully exercise our gifts, there is a guarantee here that we will receive more as a reward.

And the reward is not based on the number of talents given and the amount of increase; reward is based upon faithfulness, for the second servant received the same reward as the first, even though he was given fewer talents to begin with and only increased his gift by two more. The third servant would have received the same reward as the first two if he had but been faithful and brought back one more by way of increase.

The faithful servants were invited into the Kingdom to rule over many things, simply because they had been faithful over a few in their lifetimes. But the third servant was stripped of the one talent he had been given, and it was awarded to the one with ten talents.

What kept the third servant from doing anything profitable with his talent? It seems to be two problems: he was afraid, and he misjudged his lord.

Of what was he afraid? Of losing the only talent he had, because he thought the lord was a hard man (sounds like one who still labored under the old law and legalism). And he accused his lord of taking where he had done no work to earn anything: yet our Lord sowed His very life that eternal Life and gifts might be given to man. Burying his talent "in the ground" is also interesting; there is a hint here of worldly living, depending upon the things of the earth and not Heaven.

Finally, there is the question of the third servant's destiny. Some have said he was not even among the saved, but that is impossible: he, like the first two, was a servant of the same lord (all who are called servants of our Lord are saved ones). And the unsaved are never given the gifts of the Holy Spirit.

Others have consigned the third servant to hell, supporting their view of the possibility of losing one's salvation after a genuine conversion. They cite the place where he is sent as proof—"outer darkness, where there will be weeping and gnashing of teeth" (verse 30).

But nowhere in the Bible is hell referred to as a place of outer darkness. Indeed, compared to being with the Lord in the Kingdom, anywhere else but there will be a place of great darkness and deep regret for what could have been; hence, "weeping and gnashing of teeth."

The unprofitable servant will be sharing the same experience as the five foolish virgins, a long period of preparation required to be part of the new Heaven and new earth, which will follow the thousand-year reign of Christ and His overcomers.

The Parable of the Sheep and the Goats

> When the Son of Man comes in His glory, and all the holy angels with him, He will sit on the throne of His glory. All the nations will be scattered before Him, and He will separate them one from another, as a shepherd divides his sheep from his goats. And He will set the sheep on His right hand, but the goats on the left. Then the King will say to those on His right hand, 'Come, you blessed on My Father, inherit the kingdom prepared for you from the foundation of the world: for I was hungry and you gave Me food; I was thirsty and

you gave Me drink; I was a stranger and you took Me in; I was naked and you clothed me; I was sick and you visited Me; I was in prison and you came to Me.' Then the righteous will answer Him, saying, 'Lord, when did we see You hungry and feed You, or thirsty and give You drink? When did we see You a stranger and take You in, or naked and clothe You? Or when did we see You sick, or in prison, and come to You?' And the King will answer and say to them, 'Assuredly, I say to you, inasmuch as you did it to one of the least of these My brethren, you did it to Me.' Then He will say to those on the left hand, 'Depart from Me, you cursed into the everlasting fire prepared for the devil and his angels: for I was hungry and you gave Me no food; I was thirsty and you gave Me no drink; I was a stranger and you did not take Me in; naked and you did not clothe Me, sick and in prison and you did not visit Me.' Then they will also answer Him, saying, 'Lord, when did we see You hungry or thirsty or a stranger or naked or sick or in prison, and did not minister to You?' Then He will answer them, saying, 'Assuredly, I say to you, inasmuch as you did not do it to one of the least of these, you did not do it to Me.' And these will go away into everlasting punishment, but the righteous into eternal life.

> Matthew 25:31–46

In one sense of the word, this prophecy by the Lord is not a parable at all: for He simply foretold and explained what will happen to "the nations" as a result of their treatment of Christians and believing Jews during the Great Tribulation. Some will enter the Kingdom as flesh and blood citizens, while others will be consigned to everlasting punishment.

But just who are these who will be thus judged by the Lord? The Bible refers to three classes of people in its pages: Jews, Christians, and the nations. The same word for nations is used to refer to Gentiles, all non-Jews; and Christians, of course, are composed of both believing Jews and believing Gentiles. But the nations in this parable cannot be Christians or believing Jews, for their entrance into the Kingdom is not on the basis of grace through faith, but rather works. They seem to be uncommitted Gentiles who choose to either be kind to those being hunted and persecuted by anti-christ, or to deal with them harshly, perhaps even aiding the enemy in his pursuit of them.

The holy angels will gather the nations for their judgment, and the Lord will be in Jerusalem on His throne by that time. When He tells the righteous ones to enter into the Kingdom as a reward for their gracious and brave treatment of His brethren, they will seem not to even understand when they ever did such a thing. The unrighteous ones will likewise be baffled as to when they ignored the Lord in His need.

This is further evidence that these Gentiles are neither Jews nor Christians. The Lord identifies with even the "least" of His brothers and sisters; so He explains to both groups that when they treated His own in such a way, it was actually the same as treating or mistreating Him; and that is how they will be judged.

The fact that both the sheep and the goats will be judged by Christ on the basis of works raises the question as to the eternal state of those deemed righteous. Since eternal salvation is by faith alone, and these sheep nations are not called saved ones by the Lord, what will be their eternal destiny?

We know from Scripture that during the thousand-year reign of Christ on the earth, Satan and his fallen angels will be confined to the Abyss, or bottomless pit; they will therefore have no direct influence on the flesh and blood beings who will inhabit the Kingdom (the overcomers, who will rule and reign with Christ, will already be in their glorified form by then).

But when Satan is released from the pit at the end of the Millennium, he will go out to "deceive the nations" we are told in Revelation 20:6 and 7. This will be the time that the "sheep" will have to make their choice on the basis of faith: some will be deceived and be damned, but others will believe unto salvation and be saved. Thus all who will enter the new Heaven and new earth will do so by faith alone.

(Perhaps they are the "gleanings" from the Lord's wheat field, those gathered after the first-fruits and the main harvest; this will be discussed later under the heading of "Rapture.")

The grace and mercy of God is astounding! Here we have a group of people who will not have believed in Christ unto salvation prior to the return of the Lord, and yet they will receive another chance during the thousand years to come to a saving knowledge of the Savior! Another amazing thing to consider? For a thousand years, no one in the Kingdom will be affected by the direct temptations or attacks of Satan. There will be Christ, His overcoming saints in a glorified state, angels, and flesh-and-blood mortals, a seemingly "perfect" time; and yet many will be deceived by Satan when he is set free for a short season; how can that be?

What does that tell us about our heart and soul (self) now? How deep the roots of the tree of the knowledge of good and evil must go! The heart truly is deceitful above all things; we indeed must guard it with all diligence!

END-TIMES: THE JEWS

And Jesus answered and said to them: 'Take heed that no one deceives you. For many shall come in My name, saying, 'I am the Christ,' and deceive many. And you will hear of wars and rumors of wars. See that you are not troubled; for all these things must come to pass, but the end is not yet. For nation will rise against nation, and kingdom against kingdom. And there will be famines, pestilences, and earthquakes in various places. All these are the beginnings of sorrows. Then they will deliver you up to tribulation and kill you, and you will be hated by all nations for My name's sake. And then many will be offended, will betray one another, and will hate one another. Then many false prophets will rise up and deceive many. And because lawlessness will abound, the love of many will grow cold. But he who endures to end shall be saved. And this gospel of the Kingdom will be preached in all the world as a witness to all nations, and then the end will come. Therefore when you see the abomination of desolation, spoken of by Daniel the prophet, standing in the holy place (whoever reads, let him understand), then let those in Judea flee to the mountains. Let him who is on the housetop not go down to take anything out of the house. And let him who is in the field not go back to get his clothes. But woe to those who are pregnant and to those who are nursing babies in those days! And pray that your flight may not be in winter or on the Sabbath. For then there will be great tribulation, such as has not been since the beginning of the world until this time, no, nor ever shall be. And unless those days were shortened, no flesh would be saved; but for the elect's sake those days will be shortened. Then if anyone says to you, 'Look, here is the Christ!' or 'There!' do not believe it. For false christs and false prophets will rise and show great signs and wonders to deceive, if possible, even the elect. See, I have told you beforehand. Therefore, if they say to you, 'Look, He is in the desert!' do not go out; or 'Look, He is in the inner rooms!' do not believe it. For as the lightning comes from the east and flashes to the west, so also will the coming of the Son of Man be. For wherever the carcass is, there the eagles will be gathered together. Immediately after the tribulation of those days the sun will be darkened, and the moon will not give its light: the stars will fall from Heaven, and the powers of the Heavens will be shaken. Then the sign of the Son of Man will appear in Heaven, and then all the tribes of the earth will mourn, and they will see the Son of Man coming on the clouds of Heaven with power and great glory. And he will send His angels with a great sound of a trumpet, and they will gather together his elect from the four winds, from one end of Heaven to the other.

Matthew 24:4–31

This long passage was the first part of the answer by Jesus to the disciples' question concerning the destruction of the temple and the end of the age. In answering, He gave many signs of the end as well. The main emphasis was for the disciples to take heed and not be fooled. The things that will happen and possibly mislead many would be the coming of false christs and wars and rumors of wars.

Even in the early days following Christ's death and resurrection, while the disciples were yet alive, both of these predictions came to pass in Israel: many false messiahs came and went, and warfare greatly increased. From then to our own day, such events have multiplied, and prophets themselves have often been misled, thinking the end surely was imminent during their own lifetimes. But the Word said then, and continues to say today: "But the end is not yet" (verse 6).

We also must remember that Christ's answer from verse 4 to verse 31 was a prophecy of what will happen to the Jewish people, especially those who come to Christ. That is why such words as the "abomination of desolation," Judea, and the Sabbath were mentioned. Of course, Christians (both Jews and Gentiles) will be affected when all these things come to pass. But Jesus was primarily addressing the Jews in this part of His answer.

Next, Christ mentioned an increase in famines, pestilences, and earthquakes in various places (outside Israel as well as within); and again, those tragedies have been on the increase from the days Jesus predicted them up to the present moment. But rather than those signs signaling the end, Christ assured the disciples (and us): "All these are the beginnings of sorrows" (verse 8).

The word "sorrows" is called "travail" in other translations, as in childbirth. When a woman goes into labor, she experiences intense travail, but this is then followed by the joy of birth. Israel, Jesus seemed to be saying, will go through the same process; for next the Word says: "Then they will deliver you up to tribulation and kill you, and you will be hated by all nations for My name's sake" (verse 9).

But since even this is but the beginning of sorrows, greater tribulation will lie ahead before the "end" is reached.

Not all the Jews will come to Him, the Lord said. Instead, some will begin to hate their brethren and even betray them during their period of tribulation. The rising of false prophets, sent by the enemy for the purpose of deception, was again mentioned. And lawlessness will abound: the anti-christ is the lawless one, and his progeny and followers all live by the same principle of rebellion.

Then Jesus gave a word of encouragement:

"But he who endures to the end will be saved" (verse 13). Hallelujah!

Next came a most startling statement:

"And this gospel of the Kingdom will be preached in all the world as a witness to all the nations, and then the end will come" (verse 14).

We cannot be sure just when all the prophecy from verses 1 to 13 will be completed, but we can know this: all the events prophesied from verses 13–14 to verse 31 will take place during the last three and a half years, the period known as the Great Tribulation. Jewish believers, along with their Gentile brethren, will be preaching this Word; all overcomers, who preached and lived it *before* the Tribulation will already be gone, having been received by the Lord in rapture.

There is only one gospel, the gospel of grace. But that gospel can be viewed from different points of view: sinners are saved by grace through faith in the finished work of Jesus on the cross, but the gospel of the Kingdom has as its focus the absolute authority and sovereignty of God, which is still the gospel of grace—for it is only by grace and faith in the reality of the Life of Christ within becoming the Life of the believer that absolute obedience to the authority of God can come to pass.

Many are the saved by grace, but few are the overcomers (by the power of the gospel of the Kingdom of the Heavens). All the saved ones are not overcomers in this sense; they have overcome the penalty of sin through the shed blood of the Lord Jesus Christ, but they have not overcome self by yielding to their co-crucifixion, resurrection, and ascension with Christ. This is the position of all believers, but all do not experience it in this life. Due to aspects of self being alive and well and the deceptions of the enemy, the power of sin continues to win the battle between the flesh and the spirit in such believers.

Once this gospel of the Kingdom has been preached to all nations, the end will come. A time of horrific tribulation such as the world has never seen will precede this ending and the beginning of the Millennium. Verse 15 is given as a sure sign of the end, something every Jew should understand: "Therefore when you see the 'abomination of desolation,' spoken of by Daniel the prophet, standing in the holy place' (whoever reads let him understand) 'then let those who are in Judea flee to the mountains.'" The anti-christ will have invaded and desecrated the temple in Jerusalem. The only way of escape will be to flee, for things will become so terrible that unless the Lord shortens those days, no flesh would have survived; but praise His Name, He will shorten them for the sake of the elect!

Once again, Jesus gave a warning about false messiahs and false prophets, for they will surely appear at that time, many of them able to perform all sorts of signs and wonders. But the Lord told the disciples and us not to follow anything that resembles this counterfeit; none of them will be Him.

He then gave an exact description of how He will return, and that it will be so obvious that no one will have to wonder if it is truly Him or not: "For as the lightning comes from the east and flashes to the west, so also will the coming of the Son of Man be" (verse 26). All will witness the true coming of the Lord.

Moving on, we come to a very peculiar verse (28): "For wherever the carcass is, there the eagles will be gathered together." A carcass is a dead body, and we know that eagles eat dead flesh as part of their diet. One thing is certain at this point in the prophecy: the time of judgment will have arrived. And what is to be judged? All those who are still dead in Adam. Believers are no longer in that state, for they have died to the old man and come alive in the new man in Christ Jesus; our dead flesh, or carcass, has already been judged and condemned to death on the cross with Christ (Romans 6:6).

Putting this all together, what Jesus was saying here is this: The time will have come for the judgment of all those still "in

Adam." Judgment will have come to judge their flesh, even as an eagle devours the carcass of dead animals.

Jesus then gave another time factor in verse 29: "Immediately after the tribulation of those days the sun will be darkened, and the moon will not give its light; the stars will fall from Heaven, and the powers of the Heavens will be shaken." This is the second time such celestial calamities will occur, the first time being at the beginning of the Tribulation (see Revelation 6:12–13 and Joel 2:31). Then some sort of sign (we are not given what it will be) will also be seen in the Heavens, the "sign of the Son of Man"; all nations will see it, and the people of Israel will mourn for the One they had pierced (Zechariah 12:10).

Lastly, concluding Christ's prophecy concerning the Jews in the end-times, the angels, with a great sound of a trumpet, will gather together the elect from all corners of the earth to face the King at the judgment seat of Christ.

By the end of Matthew 25, Jesus had answered all three of the disciples' questions: when the temple would be destroyed, what would be the sign of His coming, and the end of the age. In Matthew 24:4–31, Jesus spoke mainly to the Jews concerning those things; from 24:32 to 25:30, He addressed the church; and from 25:31–46, He spoke to the church about the Gentiles (those nations outside both Judaism and Christianity).

A sure sign to the church that the end is near will be the return of life to the fig tree (Jews coming to the Messiah), and the sign to the Jews will be the rapture of at least part of the church; both events occurring *before* the Tribulation. In our own day, we are witnessing more Jews than ever before coming to Christ as Savior; this will increase as the time of the end draws nearer.

Those believers who love His appearing and have overcome the evil one and self, His Life becoming their lives, are waiting for release from their mortal shells, to be received by the Lord in what has become known as "rapture." Their being received will signal to the Jews that the time of the end is at hand.

RAPTURE

Note: Many Biblical scholars divide the seven-year period known as the Tribulation into two parts: the first three and a half years as the Tribulation, and the second three and a half years as the Great Tribulation. I use only the one word, Tribulation, to describe the entire seven-year period: certainly things will grow worse and worse, but for my purposes here I felt no need for such a division.

The rapture of the church is a very complicated issue and has become the basis for much controversy and misunderstanding among sincere believers. Some believe that no such event will ever occur. Others believe it will come to pass, but disagree on the "when-and-who." Whatever one's view of rapture might be, it should never be used as a basis for division.

Three views are prevalent concerning these things: one group believes that the whole body of the saved will be raptured before the Tribulation, another that the whole body must go through the Tribulation before they are raptured, and finally, those who believe part of the saved ones will be raptured before the Tribulation and part of them after. Rather than discuss the merits and weaknesses of each viewpoint (knowing that only one can be accurate), let us choose the interpretation we believe to be true and defend it from the Scriptures.

> Because you have kept the Word of my patience, I also will keep you from the hour of trial which shall come upon the whole world, to test those who dwell on the earth.
>
> Revelation 3:10

> Then two men will be in the field: one will be taken and the other left. Two women shall be grinding at the mill: one will be taken and the other left. Watch therefore, for you do not know what hour your Lord is coming.
>
> Matthew 24:40–42

> But concerning the times and the seasons, brethren, you have no need that I should write to you. For you yourselves know perfectly that the day of the Lord comes as a thief in the night... but you, brethren, are not in darkness, so that this Day should overtake you as a thief.
>
> 1 Thessalonians 5:1, 2, 4

Many have discounted the fact of the rapture because the word itself does not appear in the Bible. While this assertion is quite true, Scripture does speak of the process of being caught away. Rapture is actually closer in meaning to "being received" as found in John 14:1–3, in which the Lord announced that He is going to prepare a place for His own, and that He will come again to receive them to Himself.

Others have refused to believe in rapture because it was not part of early church teachings, only becoming recognized (or rediscovered) in relatively modern times. This is not a legitimate criticism, unless one totally dismisses the concept of progressive revelation on both individual and corporate levels.

When the prophet Daniel did not understand part of the prophecy revealed to him by the Holy Spirit, the "man clothed in linen" said: "Go your way, Daniel, for the words are closed up and sealed till the time of the end" (Daniel 12:9).

In other words, when it was time for such things to be made known, they would be revealed. In the same manner, the apostle Paul called "Christ in you, the hope of glory" (Colossians 1:26) an unknown mystery until it was revealed to him and now to us.

As the time of the end approaches, it is critical that all believers understand the rapture of the church; who will be received by the Lord, and when.

In Revelation, chapters 2 and 3, Jesus walked among the seven churches and in essence did a spiritual analysis of their conditions. He commended them for certain qualities and condemned them for others, commanding them to repent and make things right with God.

The church at Philadelphia was the true church in the eyes of the Lord. They were not a large, strong church; they only had a little strength, but they had been faithful to keep His Word (of patience) and had not denied His Name. For this, He promised to keep them from the Tribulation, for surely this is the only "trial which shall come upon the whole world" (3:10).

Three facts are established in this short passage: the fact of rapture, when it will take place, and who will be taken. Clearly, at least a portion of believers will be raptured before the Tribulation, which refutes the idea that all believers have to pass through the Tribulation before they are raptured. And it also strongly suggests that not all believers will be taken before the Tribulation: Philadelphia was the only church given the promise, and they only represent one-seventh of the church.

Some would argue that the seven churches are only to be understood in a literal sense, specific churches in Asia Minor at the time of John writing Revelation. But a study of church history reveals that they are indeed a picture of the entire church age. Some of the characteristics of all the churches can be found to exist at all times, even today, but the prevalent condition of each church runs parallel to the different eras of church history. Either way, it was only the church at Philadelphia that was promised to be kept from the Tribulation.

Others would argue that the "keeping from" is actually a keeping "through." This, however, is in error because the word "ek" follows keep, and ek means "out of," as in the word ekklesia (the called out ones). There are only two ways that anyone can be kept from the Tribulation: by death or by rapture; so it is self-evident that at least a part of those alive at the time of the rapture will be "received" by the Lord before the Tribulation.

Another proof that only part of the church will be raptured before the Tribulation can be found in Luke 21:36: "Watch therefore, and pray always that you may be counted worthy to escape all these things that will come to pass and to stand before the Son of Man."

Why would watchfulness and prayer be called for if all believers will be raptured before the Tribulation? We would simply wait and then go. Also "being counted worthy" to escape means a condition other than faith is required to be spared from the Tribulation. Another version of this verse says "that you might prevail." We are saved by faith alone, but rapture requires works, an effort of some kind.

Oh! How that smacks in the ears and hearts of many believers. But there is no getting around it. All ten virgins in Matthew 25 were saved ones, but only five of them were wise, having been given extra oil each time they surrendered self and their own will to the will of God. On that basis they will attend the Wedding Supper as the Bride, but the foolish ones will be kept out, not taking part at all.

The condition for pre-tribulational rapture is the same: the wise will make Christ their all-in-all, exchanging their lives for His, thereby being counted worthy and prevailing; the foolish will make no such sacrifice and will have to pass through the Tribulation before they, too, can be raptured.

One other objection is that to desire to be raptured before the Tribulation is an act of cowardice, to escape when we are needed the most, to help others through the great trial. This too is erroneous, for the same Holy Spirit who helped those who will be raptured before the Tribulation will still be working during the Tribulation. He is more than able to take care of all things for the sake of the elect at that time. Full maturity in Christ is required of all believers; some merely reach that state before others.

One last point to be considered here is the maturing process through which all believers must pass. In the Old Testament, the Father referred to His own people as grapes planted in His vineyard; but in the New, as a field of wheat (Parable of the Sower).

This is a very important distinction. Grapes are only fully ripe when their juice reaches its optimal level. Wheat on the other hand is not ripe until it is totally dried out: head, fruit, stem, and roots. Both draw their strength from the earth, but grapevines have roots that go much deeper than do the roots of wheat (this suggests the earthly part of the Kingdom promised to the Jews). But the heads of wheat point toward the Heavens, where the intense heat of the sun dries them out; hence the Heavenly promises made by Christ to all overcomers.

This is surely a picture of the maturing of believers. The sun of tribulations while on the earth is to dry us out, bringing us to "ripeness." Each time we yield to the Holy Spirit, we dry out a bit more, remaining "wet" in that area if we do not submit. And all believers, even as wheat, dry out at different rates; the moisture of self must all be removed before we are ready to be harvested.

When the time for harvest (rapture) comes, only the firstfruits will be ready for the sickle; the rest must go through more heat (tribulation) before they, too, are harvested. Hence the need for some believers to pass through the Tribulation before they are raptured.

Of course, that is the point of this entire book: to show that the eternal purpose of the Father is for His Son to be the sum of all things, all-in-all, that everything in the universe be filled with nothing but the Life and glory of Christ. Those who see that and yield to the Spirit, exchanging their lives for His, have no need to pass through the Tribulation. They are those who have overcome (Rev. 2 and 3) and who will reign with Christ during the Millennial Kingdom.

That is why the Holy Spirit works so hard now, through revelation and chastening, that all believers might be ready ahead of time.

One Picture of Rapture

The Lord sees us as wheat
Ripening in His field,
The Spirit supplying heat
To bring the highest yield.

The first-fruits reaped when dry,
All the heads turned to gold;
They are the first to die,
The first to form the fold.

Later, after the sun
Has dried both stalk and root,
The main harvest will come
To gather gilded fruit.

Gleanings are left till last
(The Lord will not forget!)
His own will not be passed,
Though last redeemed from debt.

PART 3:
THE ETERNAL PROVISIONS IN CHRIST

Thus far, we have spoken of God's eternal purpose and His plan to achieve that purpose. For His Son to become the sum of all things, two obstacles had to be overcome: the rebellion of Satan and the fall of man. The first Adam was given dominion over all things, but failed, surrendering that dominion. It required the coming of the second man (1 Cor. 15:47), even the man Jesus, to come and prevail over the devil, taking back the dominion and placing it and Himself in the spirit of all born-again believers.

Christ Himself *is* the plan. Not "things" outside Himself, but He Himself, and all that He is. "All-in-all" is an all-inclusive term, meaning that nothing of any spiritual value exists outside Christ Himself. He is my healing, He is the way, the truth, and the Life. He does not show us the way, teach us truth, ask us to live like Him. He is all three Himself. And He is everything else spiritual as well... all-in-all.

What we must now explore are the provisions within the plan that assure its success. What has the Father provided in His Son for his plan to work and achieve His eternal purpose? For unless we come to see and make use of those provisions, all the words in Scripture become just so much "pie in the sky." Spiritual truth must be grounded to have any real value; which is just another way of saying that "Christ in us" must be released for victory to come.

CRUCIFIED WITH CHRIST

…just as He chose us in Him before the foundation of the world…

Ephesians 1:4a

If any man is in Christ, he is a new creature: the old things are passed away; behold they are become new.

2 Corinthians 5:17

…knowing this, that our man was crucified with Him, that the body of sin might be done away with, that we should no longer be slaves to sin… Likewise you also, reckon yourselves to be dead indeed to sin, but alive to God in Christ Jesus our Lord.

Romans 6:6, 11

I have been crucified with Christ; it is no longer I who live, but Christ lives in me; and the life which I now live in the flesh I live by faith in the Son of God, who loved me and gave Himself for me.

Galatians 2:20

My spiritual path to the revelation of God's eternal purpose has been a long and winding one. For many years, I simply sought to improve my life, repenting of my sins and endeavoring to do well. I had no idea that such a thing is impossible. So, no matter how hard I tried, I kept failing. Joy eluded me, as did any lasting peace. In short, I became miserable. But I did not give up; I knew there had to be more.

My first major breakthrough came almost twenty years ago, when the Spirit showed me that I had been crucified with Christ (Rom. 6:6, 11). Certainly I did not understand how such a thing could be true, but there it was, right in the Word. After striving to just have faith in what those Scriptures say, but struggling, the Lord began to explain to me what it means to be "in Christ," that all we are and ever will be is only possible because we are in Him.

We tend to think in such limited ways, reason dominating what we understand and accept, forgetting that God is above time and space and without limits. He sees all things at once, knows all things, and can do all things. Placing us in Christ before the foundation of the world presented no problem for Him. On the basis of His foreknowledge, we who are His were chosen and deposited in Christ, and it is there that we enjoy every spiritual blessing and partake of God's divine nature (1 Peter 1:2, 2 Peter 1:4).

Once "in Christ," of course, we can never be taken out. For nothing can separate us from the love of Christ, and not one whom the Father has placed in Christ's hand will ever be lost (Romans 8:39, John 10:28–30). So spiritually speaking, everywhere Christ has been, we have been. That is how our "old man" was crucified. When He was crucified, we were in Him, so our old man was crucified as well.

Hallelujah! My old man, all that I was "in Adam" was consigned to the cross where my Savior died. When He died, I died! Jesus did not only die for me, but He included my old sinful self, that part separating me from God, to die with Him.

So much time is spent on the old man, trying to patch him up; seeking to fix all that went wrong in his life. This is true in most counseling efforts, Christian-based as well secular approaches. This is the path that most new believers follow as well, not knowing the futility and frustration that awaits. Some never get beyond this point in their walk. They simply "settle" for less, never realizing the immense inheritance in Christ that is theirs. Hiding this knowledge has been one of the most effective strategies of deception that the enemy has employed; and thereby preserved his position as "prince" of this world.

The revelation that the old man was judged by God to be worthy of only one thing—death by crucifixion, was quite liberating for me. I no longer had to strive in my own power to please God; He is already pleased because I am in His Son.

But of course, Satan did not let me off so easily. Just as he questioned Eve, asking, "Did God say…?" he did the same to me. As I began the process of walking in my new revelation, "reckoning" (claiming by faith) that my old man is dead, the first time I sinned, the enemy asked, "Is he really dead? Is that true? Then how did he raise his head back up again and cause you to fall into one of your old ways? No, he is still very much alive, I think."

I struggled on, reckoning I was dead every time I felt the pull of the old man; but the more I reckoned the more he seemed to be alive! Then two more revelations came that helped for a while.

If I was crucified with Christ, surely I was also raised with Him, and if resurrected, then also ascended. For if I can never be taken out of Christ, I am still in Him. Where He has been, I have been, and where He is, I am. The Word, of course, confirms these truths (Romans 6:5, Ephesians 2:6).

Such is the *position* of all those who are in Christ Jesus. Not only did we die with Him, we were also raised with Him, and "made to sit together in Heavenly places in Christ Jesus." Oh what joy flooded over me as I received this revelation! Forgiveness by His shed Blood, and now deliverance seemed at hand: no more a slave to the old man and sin. A position high above all the movements of the enemy, a view of things below as Christ sees them!

I walked and prayed in the light of this new revelation for some time; praying for God to give me His vision of things and seeking to rise above the entanglements of this life. But of course, this lofty position did not always square with my actual experience. At times there seemed to be a huge gulf between the two, and I did not know how to bridge the gap. The enemy would always return to remind me of this stark fact, stealing my sense of euphoria and peace.

I once again grew dissatisfied, which I see now was a good thing. Divine dissatisfaction is something we should never lose, at least not until Jesus comes and we are changed into our glorified state. This kind of dissatisfaction compels us onward, wanting more and more of God. For if we refuse to move on, we know we will "die" in the wilderness before we ever reach the Kingdom. God is faithful, who has promised that those who hunger and thirst after righteousness shall be filled (Matthew 5:6).

He also said, "Ask, and it will be given to you; seek, and you will find; knock, and it will be opened to you" (Matthew 7:7).

Such, if we persevere, is the Christian walk: a series of gates opening onto new ways, places where a decision must be made—do I enter and walk this new way, or do I stop here? The gate is not always a pleasant one (the price to enter is often high, for another part of self must be left behind if we are to enter), and the way that will follow is not always clear.

That is where divine dissatisfaction comes in: it causes us to ask and ask until God answers; then on the basis of what is given, we seek and seek. Eventually we find what we are seeking, which brings us a bit closer to our goal. Finally, we stand at the very door (gate) and knock. We have found what we asked for and sought; it only remains for us to enter and walk on the new path God has arranged for us. But do we dare go in?

CHRIST IN US

> ...the mystery which has been hidden from ages and from generations, but now has been revealed to His saints. To them God willed to make known what are the riches of the glory of this mystery among the Gentiles: which is Christ in you, the hope of glory.
>
> Colossians 1:26–27

> I have been crucified with Christ; it is no longer I who live, but Christ lives in me; and the life which I now live in the flesh I live by faith in the Son of God, who loved me and gave Himself for me.
>
> Galatians 2:20

These two Scriptures were the next gate I came to as I hungered and thirsted for more and more of God. I was teaching a young couple who had just come to Christ, trying to help them build a solid foundation in the faith. I came to Galatians 2:20, a familiar passage, and started to expound on it when a peculiar feeling rushed over me. I could hardly finish teaching, so powerful was the sensation. After praying and sending the new converts on their way, I sought the Lord for what He was trying to tell me.

When I say, "The Lord told me..." I do not mean I heard His voice audibly, but in my spirit I heard Him say, speaking of Galatians 2:20, "That is not you, son. You can teach all about it quite well, but it is not who you are." As I was meditating on that, in total agreement, I heard Him add: "You don't really know anything unless it is who you are."

While I realized that my grasp of my co-crucifixion, -resurrection and -ascension with Christ was only my position, but not yet my actual experience, it took me awhile to understand the Lord's second statement. But then a deeper understanding began to dawn: the whole purpose of revelational knowledge is to transform us; otherwise it is just so much "head" knowledge, teaching with no practical value.

So, I then embarked on a search for the transformation inherent in Galatians 2:20: exchanging my life for His. Not really knowing where to start, I just let the revelation sort of simmer on the back burner of my spirit, waiting on the Lord for direction. In His own timing, the Spirit led me to Colossians 1:26–27, again a portion of Scripture with which I was quite familiar.

But He warned me at this point that familiarity can often rob us of real meaning. We memorize Scripture, which is a good thing, but often in that very process, we lose the essence of what the Spirit is saying. So as I read those two verses, I did so with "new eyes," so to speak.

Instead of getting to "Christ in you, the hope of glory," and thinking in my heart something like, Praise God, hallelujah! I restrained my reaction and meditated on what I had just read. Mystery—something not previously known. Never until the Spirit revealed it to Paul, and he in turn to us, had this ever been known.

Again, progressive revelation, no need for all the great men of God in the Old Testament to know it. Christ living in us! This is the key, I thought. Jesus not only died for us, and we with Him, but He also has taken up residence in our spirits to live His Life through us. This is the only hope for deliverance and victory.

THE ETERNAL PURPOSE, RESTATED

And He put all things under His feet, and gave Him to be head over all things to the church, which is His body, the fullness of Him who fills all-in-all.

Ephesians 1:22–23

He who descended is also the One who ascended far above all the Heavens, that He might fill all things.

Ephesians 4:10

...where there is neither Greek nor Jew, circumcised nor uncircumcised, barbarian, Scythian, slave nor free, Christ is all and in all.

Colossians 3:11

Now when all things are made subject to Him, then the Son Himself will also be subject to Him who put all things under Him, that God may be all-in-all.

1 Corinthians 15:28

All the pieces of the mystery were beginning to fall into place. I began to see what is the eternal purpose of God, the reason for everything that exists. And I had already understood part of the plan and provision to achieve His ordained purpose. It would have been simpler (and taken less time!) if I had known the purpose first, but it did not happen that way. But God is faithful: after showing me the pieces, He began to put them together for me.

As I have stated previously, the eternal purpose is that Christ be all-in-all, the sum of all things, everything in existence filled with nothing but the Life and glory of His Son. When that revelation is fully grasped, it changes everything. Nothing besides Christ and His Life becoming our life matters anymore. No more fruitless attempts to be like Him, no more striving after anything outside Him; the realization that outside Him, nothing of any spiritual value exists.

No need to read thick tomes on holiness, etc., etc., etc. He is holiness; die to self and let Him come forth; that is holiness. Anything else is man-made, and the same is true for every other "spiritual" virtue. Anything else is a mixture, preventing Him from being the fullness that fills all things.

So much emphasis is placed on salvation, being born-again by faith in the shed Blood of the Lord Jesus. And indeed this is crucial, for without new birth, nothing that follows is possible. But too little emphasis is placed on growing to maturity in Christ; and much of what is taught in this area is no more than trying to reform the old man and make a Christian of him. Co-death, resurrection, and ascension remain a mystery to most believers; and those who do learn these precious truths do not know how to turn them into reality. And position without experience is fruitless.

The good news is that the Father has made a way for us to make that translation. Satan has been very good at keeping the process a secret, but within the plan, provisions have been included to make our position in Christ our experience if we are willing to pay the price. Jesus made the Father all-in-all during His time upon the Earth as the second man and last Adam, thereby taking back the dominion over all things that was given away by the first Adam. His Life, deposited within the spirits of all born-again believers, includes that dominion, even dominion over Satan. The willing yielding of our new Life in Christ to the Life of Christ, a spiritual exchange taking place, releases the One who has already defeated Satan. Then victory is certain. This is the way we overcome; there is no other. Overcome the penalty of sin, the power of sin, and the Law, that Christ might be all-in-all.

ESSENTIAL FOOD

> Your lamb shall be without blemish, a male of the first year... the whole assembly of the congregation of Israel shall kill it at twilight. And they shall take some of the blood and put it on the two doorposts and on the lintel of the houses where they eat it. Then they shall eat the flesh on that night; roasted in fire, with unleavened bread and with bitter herbs they shall eat it...
>
> Exodus 12:5, 7, 8

When a sinner comes to Christ as Savior, he is called to leave both the world and sin behind. This is beautifully illustrated in the Old Testament exodus of the Israelites from Egypt. Moses had been commissioned by God for this task of deliverance. But in spite of many miraculous signs, Pharaoh had refused to let the people go. One final plague was about to fall: the death of the first-born. The death angel would pass over the land, and all the first-born of both man and beast would die.

To protect His own people from the plague, however, the Lord gave them very explicit instructions: they were to choose a year-old lamb, without blemish, to kill it at twilight, place its blood above the doorposts and lintels; then eat it that night, roasted, with bitter herbs and unleavened bread. They were to eat it all in haste, for their journey out of Egypt was imminent.

The Lord Jesus is the spotless Lamb, without sin, sacrificed for our sins so that we will not be touched by the second death (the lake of fire). This is the meaning of the blood spread along the doorposts and lintels of the houses that night: the death angel would see the blood and "pass over" that dwelling and those inside.

But there was also the matter of leaving Egypt. Egypt in Scripture is almost always synonymous with the concept of "the world," the world created by the enemy, the world system. We were natural-born citizens of that world, but upon salvation, we are to leave it behind; to be in the world but not of the world. Our Kingdom is no longer part of this world once we become believers in Christ. So in type, that is exactly what the Israelites were doing that night in Exodus 12.

But to leave Egypt (the world) behind, they had to do three things: eat the lamb, prepared with bitter herbs, and eat unleavened bread with what became known as the Passover meal. The lamb of course pointed to Christ; it (He) had to be "in them" as the very strength they would need for the journey ahead. Without taking it (Him) inside them, they would never make it out of Egypt. But even that was not enough: they also had to eat the bitter herbs and unleavened bread. None of the three could be left out if they were to succeed in their departure from slavery in Egypt.

In type and shadow, eating the lamb pictures "Christ in us," the hope of glory. This is basic, foundational: without the living reality of Christ in us, failure to leave the world behind is certain. But this crucial truth has been somehow hidden by the enemy, which leaves new believers trying to forsake the world and the things of the world in *their own strength.*

What is even worse, some do not even include leaving the world behind as part of their message of salvation! So as a result, many new believers take at least part of the world with them into their new Life in Christ; or they pick and choose among the things of the world, avoiding those they deem "bad" but indulging in others they decide are all right. The Word of God, however, is quite clear on this issue:

"Do not love the world or the things in the world. If anyone loves the world, the love of the Father is not in him" (1 John 2:15). The same apostle also declared that "the whole world lies in the evil one," meaning Satan, who, along with fallen man, has created the current world.

In addition to Christ in them as their very Life-strength, they were also to eat bitter herbs and unleavened bread. Both of these items pointed to sin: the bitter herbs being representative of past sins, which had put them into bondage to the Egyptians in the first place. The eating of the herbs was both a reminder and a deep repentance for those sins.

The unleavened bread, on the other hand, stood for present sins, those transgressions they were guilty of committing even at the moment of their deliverance (salvation). They too had to be repented of and left behind.

How clearly this pointed to our own salvation in Christ: it is only by the strength of His Life within, and spirit-deep repentance for both past and present sins that we can ever truly leave the world and sin behind and make our way toward the Kingdom. The church today has grown lax and tolerant of sin within its very walls. An unscriptural form of easy belief has crept in: just be sorry for your sins and believe in Jesus and you're all right. It's okay if you still live with your girlfriend, bring her along and we'll get her saved too, everything will work out by and by... etc., etc., etc.!

How far below the true gospel message we have fallen; to a "form" of godliness with no power.

ESSENTIAL FOOD II

And when the layer of the dew lifted, there, on the surface of the wilderness, was a small round substance, as fine as frost on the ground. So when the children of Israel saw it, they said to one another, 'What is it?' For they did not know what it was. And Moses said to them. 'This is the bread which the Lord has given you to eat.'

Exodus 16:14, 15

And the Lord said to Moses, 'Go on before the people, and take with you some of the elders of Israel. Also take in your hand your rod with which you struck the water, and go. Behold, I will stand before you there on the rock in Horeb; and you shall strike the rock, and water will come out of it, that the people may drink.' And Moses did so in the sight of the elders of Israel.

Exodus 17:5, 6

Coming out of Egypt was but the beginning of their journey to Canaan for the children of Israel. They then faced a vast wilderness to pass through! Such a desert offered little in the way of food and almost no potable water. The provisions they took from Egypt were soon exhausted.

After the people cried out to Moses for meat to eat, the Lord overlooked their complaints and sent them quails at twilight and manna early the next morning. This was to indeed "test" the people and prove to them that it was He who had delivered them from Egypt.

This "bread from Heaven" was quite strange to the people; they had never seen anything like it. "What is it?" they said when they saw it, which is the literal meaning of the word "manna." The Word tells us that it was like "white coriander seed, and the taste of it was like wafers made with honey" (Exodus 16:31b).

They were to gather just enough for each day; if they gathered more than that amount, it would rot and turn to worms. On the sixth day, they could gather twice as much, so there would be food for the Sabbath, the day they were not allowed to do the work of gathering. From the morning manna first appeared until they came to the border of Canaan, this was their food; for forty years they ate manna.

Of course, after a while they grew tired of the same old thing every day. They not only bitterly complained to Moses about the situation, but some even wanted to return to Egypt! At least there they had the fleshpots, leeks, and onions, savory food to their fill.

Such longing was a clear indication that they suffered from selective recall, "forgetting" that they had also been slaves back in Egypt! So many today suffer from the same malady: they yearn to return to the world and their old ways, remembering well the pleasures of sin for a season, but forgetting the slavery that such a life involves.

Water was also in short supply, so the Lord God once again met the needs of His people. He instructed Moses to take some of the elders, and the rod with which he had struck the waters in Egypt, turning it into blood (nothing back there but death, people!), to go to a place called Horeb and strike the rock with his rod. Water would pour forth, the Lord promised, and of course that is exactly what happened when Moses obeyed God.

Now, what we must understand here is that these things were given as examples for us. We too must pass through a wilderness on our way from the world to the Kingdom; and we too need "food and water" along the way. The questions are, what is to be our manna, and what is to be our water from the rock? Both are essential if we are to complete our journey successfully.

Manna, our spiritual food, can come to us in many ways. Certainly reading the Word daily can be manna; the Bible is even called the Bread of Life. But when and how is it truly spiritual sustenance? Most of the time, our Bible reading is a matter of study, even as it should be; we are commanded to study and rightly divide its meaning. But understanding what it says does not make it manna.

Simply (but consciously) taking it in as food, eating our daily portion, whether we understand it perfectly or not, makes it manna for us. Long before nutritionists and chemists knew exactly what it is in different foods that sustain life and health (certain vitamins and minerals, etc.), people ate it, and it nourished them. Such should be our approach to the Word: it is actual food for our spirits and should be "eaten" daily!

Prayer can also be manna for a believer, but again not just any kind of prayer. Self-centered prayer has little or no "food value." The Father desires God-centered prayer, His will, not our own, being our primary concern.

The so-called "Lord's Prayer" is a great example of this type of prayer. The Father has many things He wishes to release from Heaven to earth, but He will not do so until someone prays it forth. He also promised us that so many things we worry and pray about will be "added" if we simply seek first the Kingdom and His righteousness.

Of course, to wait upon Him and His will to be made known to us often takes time. But these kind of quiet times with the

Lord are essential; to wait expectantly for the revelation of His will, but also to receive the food for our spirits that is richly supplied by all such efforts. When Jesus often went apart from the apostles for times of prayer, I believe it was this type of waiting and praying that He did: to learn and pray the Father's will and to be strengthened for the challenges that were yet ahead.

Water is even more essential than food (we can survive for three weeks or more without eating, but only three to four days with no water). In the exodus from Egypt, Moses was told by God to strike the rock at Horeb and water would come forth for the people to drink. This was surely a picture pointing to Jesus being the Rock who was struck once, releasing the Water of the Holy Spirit. Precious water in the desert! For drinking, bathing, and being refreshed, supplying strength and well-being to continue the journey.

That same water is spiritually released to all those who praise and worship the Lord in Spirit and in truth; those who walk in the Spirit and not in the flesh. Jesus told the Samaritan woman at the well in John 4: "Whoever drinks of this water will thirst again, but whoever drinks of the water that I shall give him will never thirst. But the water that I shall give him will become in him a fountain of water springing up into everlasting life" (verses 13 and 14).

We agree wholeheartedly with the woman when she answered, "Sir, give me this water..." Which He does to all who believe!

Bread and water are enough to sustain life as we journey through the wilderness from the cross to the Kingdom. But two more ingredients are needed: joy and power. Just surviving is simply not enough; day after day in the wilderness is taxing, and challenges arise that need supernatural power to overcome.

David once cried out for the Lord to restore the joy of His salvation. True, David's cry came after his sin with Bathsheba, but there are times when a surge of joy is desperately needed by all believers following after the Lord. The way becomes dark and difficult for even the most devoted: Satan buffets, brethren misunderstand each other, tribulation comes because of the Word, the Heavens seem closed to prayer.

Jesus suffered all these afflictions and countless more besides; plus the knowledge that He would be carrying the weight of the sins of the whole world as He went to the Cross was always before His face. And yet the Word says: "…looking unto Jesus, the author and finisher of our faith, who for the joy that was set before Him endured the cross, despising the shame, and has sat down at the right hand of the throne of God" (Hebrews 12:2).

He saw the end, where it was all going, the Kingdom, God's eternal purpose achieved, and that was enough to endure all things thrown at him by Satan and sinful men; not only endure them, but to do so with great joy!

Because Christ is in us, so is His joy, the same joy we can draw on in times of trouble and discouragement. Nehemiah 8:10 declares: "…Do not sorrow, for the joy of the Lord is your strength." His joy is our strength. Simply ask Him for it, taking all thoughts captive that are weighing us down, giving them to Him, then asking that His joy come forth to give us the strength to go on. He will never fail to deliver what we ask for, believing, in such situations.

"All-in-all" includes His joy!

Another place in the Scriptures where the Holy Spirit took me, to drive home this point, was Deuteronomy 32:13. Moses had just been informed that he was not going to be allowed to go over into Canaan. Instead of pleading his case or becoming bitter, Moses wrote what has become known as the Song of Moses. In part of it, he reminded the people just how gracious the Lord had been to them. Part of his praise reads: "…He made him draw honey from the rock, and oil from the flinty rock." (Another version reads, "suck" honey from the rock!)

Christ is the Rock, and the honey is joy. Honey is not a strict requirement in the physical diet; it is a little something extra, more like dessert, something that gives a sense of well-being and satisfaction; sweetness extracted from hard rock!

When Jonathan and his men ate a bit of honey (against the strict orders of his father, King Saul), it brightened their eyes and supplied the strength to continue the battle. On a spiritual level, it will do the same for us. We need not only manna and water from the Rock, but also frequent portions of joy! Christ Himself is all three.

James began his letter to the "twelve tribes which are scattered abroad" (verse 1) with these stirring words: "My brethren, count it all joy when you fall into various trials, knowing that the testing of your faith produces patience. But let patience have its perfect work, that you may be perfect and complete, lacking nothing" (James 1:2–4).

There was a time I found it very difficult to actually experience this great truth. When trials came, it was more like "grin and bear it," but certainly not counting it all joy! Satan would come to discourage. Other people (even brethren) were used by the enemy to cause me to think my pursuit of God was futile, that I was going "too far," that I should learn to relax and rest in the finished work of Christ.

But once the eternal purpose of God was revealed to me, I began to do just that: count it all joy. When difficulties arose, I saw them as an opportunity to share in the sufferings of the Lord and to rejoice in that great privilege.

Nothing happens to those who are His without the Father's knowledge; and therefore for their good and His glory. At times tribulation and persecution come to test and strengthen our faith; at other times to rid us of some of the carnal dross that prevents Christ from being all-in-all in our lives.

The Holy Spirit intends for trials to produce patience, which allows us to keep the "word of His patience" (Rev. 3:10), for once again, He is our patience; and also the "perfect work" that results. However, it is not until Christ is truly all-in-all that we will "lack nothing": Oh, what joy that revelation gives!

There is also the matter of power. For as Paul said in 1 Corinthians 4:20, "For the kingdom is not in word but in power."

By this, of course, Paul meant the foretaste of the "power of the age to come" (Hebrews 6:5) is not just a matter of talk, but of the demonstration of power confirming the Word. More than once, Paul reminded the recipients of his epistles that he did not come to them with eloquent words and great speaking prowess, but "in Spirit and in power." Power should always accompany and confirm the Word of the Kingdom.

In Matthew 12, the Jews accused Jesus of driving out demons by the power of Satan (Beelzebub). After showing how illogical and self-defeating such a thing would be, Jesus said these powerful words: "And if I cast out demons by Beelzebub, by whom do your sons cast them out? Therefore they shall be your judges. And if I cast out demons by the Spirit of God, surely the kingdom of God has come upon you" (Matthew 12:27, 28).

The Spirit of God will always confirm the true Word of the Kingdom spoken by those under the authority of the Spirit. The powerful authority Jesus demonstrated came from one source: because He Himself was under the absolute authority of the Father. The same holds true for all believers: any authority granted them is in direct proportion to their submission to the authority of Christ.

That is why Christ becoming "all-in-all" is so critical! Power is needed, if only a "foretaste" of the power of the age to come; otherwise the Word of the Kingdom is no more than just another teaching.

Returning to Deuteronomy 32:13, we find that not only are we allowed to "suck" honey (joy) from the Rock, we also are granted the privilege of drawing oil from the flinty rock. This is surely a reference to the fire (power) of the Holy Spirit. Two pieces of flint struck together just right in the presence of oil produces fire.

Jesus is the Rock from which the shards of flint are taken, believers who are His, living (or lively) stones: "Coming to Him as a living stone, rejected indeed by men, but chosen by God and precious, you also, as living stones, are being built up a spiritual house, a holy priesthood, to offer up spiritual sacrifices acceptable to God through Jesus Christ" (1 Peter 2:5).

The oil is the anointing of the Holy Spirit; and sparks plus oil means fire!

This power comes about in a number of ways. At the moment of salvation, the Word plus faith produces conviction of sin and new Life in Christ. Later, in the maturing process of the believer, these same two elements come together again and again, the mixing of faith with new revelations of the Holy Spirit, bringing repentance and burning out a bit more of whatever stands in the way of Christ becoming all-in-all.

All these benefits are "us-ward" so to speak, but the same fire is kindled outward from us as living stones of testimony, producing power as evidence of the Lordship of Christ and the coming Kingdom. Anytime we truly make His will our will, power is produced to meet whatever situation in which we may find ourselves. This is true in all spheres of our walk in Christ: teaching, healing, Words of wisdom or knowledge, Words of prophecy.

His will and ours being as one will always produce some manifestation of power, being on earth even as it is in Heaven. "Fire" is needed to burn out the old and bring forth the new, making room for more of Christ and less of us. Obedience to the Holy Spirit will always produce the necessary power to meet any situation.

In Matthew 18, Jesus makes a precious promise to all true followers:

> Assuredly, I say to you, whatever you bind on earth will be bound in Heaven, and whatever you loose on earth will be loosed in Heaven. Again I say to you that if two of you agree on earth concerning anything that they

ask, it will be done for them by My Father in Heaven. For where two or three are gathered together in My name, I am there in the midst of them.

Matthew 18:18, 19

Here we find the perfect elements for power (fire). Two or three coming together "in His Name," not merely meeting to pray for whatever comes to mind; but discerning what the Father desires to release from Heaven and as one praying it forth. Power from Heaven to earth and earth to Heaven will be the result!

Of course, in a strict sense, the fire (power) produced by the Holy Spirit is not so much food as it is evidence that the rest of our spiritual diet is complete and *working*. But that working produces faith that our path is true and that the Lord is with us. And *that* faith does become food and strength for the challenges to come, the food of increased confidence.

To make it through the wilderness to Canaan, all these are essential foods: Bread from Heaven, water, joy, and power from the Rock, remembering that it is Christ in us and us in Him that supplies our every need and gives us the victory. Neglect any of this Heavenly nutrition, and we will die in the wilderness, even as did all but Caleb and Joshua from among that multitude who were delivered from Egypt in the days of Moses. Let us take heed from those sad examples, who attempted but failed to complete the journey from Egypt (the world) to Canaan (the Kingdom).

COMMUNION

Then Jesus said to them, 'Most assuredly, I say to you, unless you eat the flesh of the Son of Man and drink His blood, you have no life in you. Whoever eats My flesh and drinks My blood has eternal life, and I will raise him up at the last day. For My flesh is food indeed, and My blood is drink indeed.'"

John 6:53–55

Take, eat; this is My body which is broken for you; do this in remembrance of Me... This cup is the new covenant in My blood. This do, as often as you drink it, in remembrance of me" (1 Cor. 11:24, 25)... "But let a man examine himself, and so let him eat of the bread and drink of the cup.

1 Corinthians 11:28

Communion is something the enemy has stolen from most of the church. For it too is real food (food indeed) and real drink (drink indeed). I did not include it in the previous discussion of essential food because it warrants special treatment of its own. How and why has the enemy stolen the real benefits of this precious provision of the Lord?

Satan knows that the bread and the wine taken in remembrance of the Lord are powerful food and drink, so he has worked very hard to cut off this source of strength. Jesus Himself said that it is real nourishment, that without it we have no life in us. There is something critical here for us to understand. In what way is the bread and wine of Communion real food and drink, what exactly did Jesus mean?

When the Holy Spirit first arrested my attention with these verses, I sought the Lord for an explanation. What I received was this: man tends to think in either-or terms; love or hate, positive or negative, good or evil. But there is what the Lord called a "spiritual reality" to many things in the Spirit that is neither one or the other. The benefits of Communion have just such a spiritual reality.

Properly discerned and taken, the bread and the wine are spiritual food and drink; they strengthen our spirit and weaken our flesh. And as the spirit grows stronger and the flesh wanes, we are enabled to better walk in the spirit (Spirit) and avoid the temptations of the flesh, all of which gradually results in Christ becoming all-in-all in our lives.

Hence, Satan's deception and thievery: the last thing he wants is for any believer to reach this level of maturity; it threatens his very existence!

How has he stolen the true meaning and benefit of Communion from the church? Again, the either-or shell game. Most Protestants only celebrate the Lord's Supper a few times a year, calling the bread and the wine symbols of His Body and Blood. There is no life in symbols! And by only occasionally taking Communion, they are starving their spirits of crucial nourishment.

Our Catholic friends, on the other hand, turn the celebration into some sort of magic show: they believe that when the priest blesses the "emblems," they are literally changed into the actual Body and Blood of Christ in a process known as transubstantiation.

Neither understanding touches the true spiritual reality of Communion. For Jesus did not say, "The bread and the wine *stand* for my body and blood," nor did He say, "They *become* my Body and Blood." He said, "For my flesh *is* real food and my blood *is* real drink." There is a great mystery here that, once revealed, gives the believer a great advantage in the process of making Christ all-in-all and thereby achieving God's eternal purpose.

Satan has always done everything in his power to weaken the Body of Christ, and this stealing of the true meaning of Communion has been one of the main means to that end. But in these last days, the Holy Spirit is uncovering the deceptions of the enemy. We must pray that more and more of the Body will have ears to hear what the Spirit is saying to the church on this essential matter.

It is very interesting that Jesus gave this teaching early in His ministry, long before the last meal with His disciples. He had just performed many miracles, including the feeding of the five thousand. Multitudes were following Him. But the Lord knew men's hearts. He knew that most of these "followers" were there for the food and the miracles. Men are always attracted to displays of the supernatural. So, to separate true followers from the false, Jesus gave this difficult teaching about the need to eat His flesh and drink His blood. After that, most of His disciples no longer stayed with Him: "From that time many of His disciples went back and walked with Him no more," reads John 6:66.

But of course His true disciples stayed, for when the Lord asked them if they would leave Him, too, Peter answered, "Lord, to whom shall we go? You have the words of eternal life" (verse 68).

Many there are who fall away when the going gets rugged or when the demands of the Lord seem rigid or incomprehensible; but the truly committed follow no matter what.

One more comment concerning the taking of Communion: the exhortation by Paul in 1 Corinthians 11 that a man should examine himself before partaking. The enemy has deceived many into believing that this means we are to check and see if our current behavior has been good enough for us to take part in Communion; if we are worthy. This could not be further from the truth, for no one is worthy enough to eat and drink at the Lord's table. The whole ceremony, in fact, is to teach us that only Christ is worthy.

Thinking themselves unworthy, so many skip taking in desperately needed spiritual food and thereby become even weaker. The time of examination is for the Holy Spirit to point out any areas of sin in need of repentance, so that we might partake with a clean conscience; even a time to admit to the Father our weakness and great need for the perfection of Christ to nourish us.

We should also praise Him for His overcoming love and sacrifice, our love for Him growing, our willingness to sacrifice all for Him increasing. It is also a perfect time to remember the Father's eternal purpose, and in deeper consecration, giving ourselves to it.

Communion means mutual participation, an act of sharing, and that is exactly what it is to be: first and foremost our mutual participation with the Living Christ; we share with Him mutual love as we remember what He has done for us, strengthening our bond and union with Him, and secondly, it binds us closer together to our brothers and sisters that make up our part of the Body of Christ.

So much is gained when His Body and Blood are properly discerned and taken. The enemy suffers great loss, and the coming Kingdom draws a bit closer. O, that the church would return to the true meaning and draw upon the power of the Lord's Supper!

TWO WILDERNESSES

We have spoken of Israel's deliverance from Egypt and have noted the similarity to our own salvation: forgiveness by God and leaving the world and sin behind. Ancient Egypt, even as our world today, was a place of great earthly achievement and opulence. But the glories of both worlds are the products of Satan and fallen man. Compared to the Garden and man's ordained purpose, it is no exaggeration to call both Egypt and our world today a wilderness from which we are to flee; to declare as Jesus did: "My kingdom is not of this world," and to live accordingly.

But the wilderness of this world is intimately connected to a second wilderness we must overcome if we are to make it to Canaan (the Kingdom): the wilderness of self. Having lived so long by the power of the soul (reason, feelings, and control), this second desert place presents a bigger challenge than the first. The only world the soul had ever known, prior to salvation, was this world. This world had been home, a place that had pampered and satisfied the soul and its desires. So the soul strives to stay in control, even after the spirit comes to life and sees a new path to take.

Israel's forty years in the wilderness after leaving Egypt is a picture of this second battle; a period of testing, a time to show who the people would trust, themselves or God. It is a matter of great sadness and tragedy that of the original group who left Egypt, only two made it to Canaan; a sobering thought indeed.

Those who fell in the desert simply could not mix faith with the Word of the Lord. Hebrews 4 warns us not to fall for the same reason and be numbered with those who fail to enter His rest. The spirit will not force its way onto the throne of our lives. We must come to a place of revelation and willing surrender to the Life of the Lord within. That is what Jesus meant when He said: "For whoever desires to save his life will lose it, but whoever loses his life for my sake will find it" (Matthew 16:25).

The word Jesus used for "life" was psuche, the Greek word for soul. We must be willing to give up the soul life in favor of the Life of the Spirit if we are to inherit the Kingdom. Those who are willing to make this sacrifice are indeed the overcomers of Revelation 2 and 3, the wise virgins of Matthew 25, and the Shulamite maiden in the Song of Solomon: those who make Christ all-in-all, no matter the cost to the soul.

The reasons to fail are many. A study of the wilderness crossing by the children of Israel reveals some of the obstacles. First, there is the matter of ignorance, simply not knowing that any such change is necessary. Most believers follow the same path: trying to forsake evil and follow the way of goodness; but they do it in their own power, failure becoming inevitable. This group often does not discover that there is anything more in the Christian walk.

Others are given revelations by the Spirit that the Lord died for more than forgiveness of sins and making a way to Heaven. They begin to see that He died to destroy the works of the devil, and called us to follow Him in this great purpose. But they do not see how that is possible, never grasping the key provisions in Christ that ensure success. Going any further seems too difficult, so they decide to "just do their best," instead of battling for the Kingdom.

Of course the pull of the flesh and the world prove too much for another group; there are just too many rigid demands, too many things to give up to follow the path of true discipleship.

In some areas, they choose to enjoy certain sins and "pleasures of Egypt for a season," rather than live a life of consecration unto the Lord. Besides, they complain, don't some people just carry this whole thing too far?

Gary Wilkerson, in a recent article in his father's "World Challenge Pulpit Series," spoke of this very process and the reasons why so many fail: "We all have a high calling from the Lord. And at various stages of our lives, he has set before us a preordained plan we are to fulfill. Moreover, God promises that if we act in faith, trusting him, he will bring that plan to fulfillment.

"Yet this isn't always easy. As everyone who has walked with Jesus for any length of time knows, following his high calling means we're going to meet obstacles. And one of the most common obstacles is the *skeptic's voice*. As we seek to cross the Jordan into the promised land, we'll hear every kind of voice telling us not to go.

These voices tell us, in very reasonable tones, 'It's just not going to happen. Let me explain to you why.'

Three types of skeptical voices appear in the life of every Christian:

First, there is the *outward skeptic*. This is a friend, acquaintance, or family member who challenges what we believe we're to do to obey God.

There is also a *demonic skeptic*. This is the voice of the evil one, who seeks to derail us from our trust in the Lord.

Finally, there is an *inner skeptic*. This is the voice inside our own minds that raises every kind of argument against obeying what God has asked of us."

Mr. Wilkerson went on to use the story of Joshua as an example of facing the voices of all three skeptics and overcoming by crossing over the Jordan in spite of opposition from all sides. He then listed seven common reasons for failure in our God-given task:

- It's easier where you are.
- It's going to take too much effort.
- Some people won't like it.
- It's physically impossible.
- It's too risky.
- If you don't succeed, you'll be ridiculed.
- Once you cross over, the struggles will never end.

All of these obstacles (and more besides) will certainly arise to prevent us from our preordained, eternal purpose. But we must have faith in the promises of Christ and know that because He has gone before us, a sure way has been made.

Most, if not all, of the reasons to quit short of the goal are fear-based. In fact, most all sins come about because of fear. But the Word says that "perfect love casts out fear" (1 John 4:18) and that "God has not given a spirit of fear, but of power, and of love and of a sound mind" (2 Timothy 1:7).

It is a terrible tragedy that so many who choose to follow the Lord end up "dying in the wilderness." They leave the world (as best they can) but never make it to Canaan. Christ has already destroyed the works of the devil, and He has put that victory in the spirit of every born-again believer. And He has given us a way to access and release that victory so that *we too* might defeat the enemy and usher in the Kingdom. In the meanwhile, let us hear the voice of Joshua stirring the people to advance over the Jordan into the promised land: "Be strong and of good courage... only be strong and courageous... have I not commanded you? Be strong and of good courage; do not be afraid, nor be dismayed, for the Lord your God is with you wherever you go" (Joshua 1:6, 7, 9).

We must not fail the Lord!

FOUNDATIONS

…you are God's building. According to the grace of God which was given to me, as a wise master builder I have laid the foundation, and another builds on it. But let each one take heed how he builds on it. For no other foundation can anyone lay than that which is laid, which is Jesus Christ. Now if anyone builds on this foundation with gold, silver, precious stones, wood, hay, straw, each one's work will become clear; for the Day will declare it, because it will be revealed by fire; and the fire will test each one's work, of what sort it is. If anyone's work which he built on it endures, he will receive a reward. If anyone's work is burned, he will suffer loss; but he himself will be saved, yet so as through fire.

1 Corinthians 3:9–15

Jesus said to them, 'Have you never read in the Scriptures: The stone which the builders rejected has become the chief cornerstone. This was the Lord's doing, and it is marvelous in our eyes.'

Matthew 21:42

Recently, the Lord brought to my attention the subject of "foundations," as it relates to individual lives, families, churches, and nations. That which something is built upon is a matter of extreme importance. If the foundation is faulty, then the whole structure that it supports will be faulty. And even if the foundation is solid, the building can still turn out wrong if the materials of its construction are defective.

The apostle Paul saw this as a developing problem in the church at Corinth, and strongly admonished the believers there to be careful about how they built upon the one sure foundation, Christ. There were already factions and divisions in the church: the people had their favorite "fathers in the faith"—some favored Apollos, others Cephas, and still others Paul. There were lawsuits, pitting one believing brother against another. An actual case of incest was taking place within the church and nothing was being done about it by the elders or members. Several other equally serious practices were occurring and being tolerated, including a profaning of the Lord's Supper.

Paul reminded the Corinthians that he had very carefully laid the foundation of their faith, Christ Jesus, but that some were building on that foundation with carnal materials. And he warned them that whatever was being used to build with will one day be judged.

At the judgment seat of Christ, all the works we have done as believers, especially those done in His Name, will be tested by "fire." Only those built by gold, silver, or precious stones will pass through the fire and come out the other side and be rewarded. Works of wood, straw, and hay will be consumed by the fire of judgment.

What will be the standard of judgment when we stand before Christ? Only one thing of course: Christ Himself! For any "work" to pass through the intense heat of His righteousness, three areas must pass the test: the origin, the process, and the glory of success. So many "good" works have been done that neither Christ nor the Holy Spirit had anything to do with; they were simply the well-intentioned ideas of man. These fall into the realm of wood, hay, and straw and will not endure.

Where did the idea or revelation for a work originate, from the heart of God or the mind of man? This question of origin is critical. For any work that does not start with a move of the Holy Spirit is doomed to failure in the eyes of the Lord. It may result in apparent success in the eyes of man: a huge church may develop, even as in the parable of the mustard seed; but quality is much more important to God than quantity. Numbers do not equal success. And unnatural growth, a small mustard bush transforming into a huge tree, is not the work of God.

Satan also sowed the seeds of tares, producing his own "sons," who infiltrated the church with heresies and false teachings, leaven, and worked it into the true lump of three measures of flour, corrupting the whole loaf. Inward corruption led to abnormal growth, both tactics of the enemy in an attempt to corrode or change the foundation.

But finding the true foundation is unchangeable, our foe worked on the building materials, even the sons and daughters of the Lord, the living stones; anything to weaken the structure of the house. The devious and diligent work of the devil has affected both the origin and the process of any effort done for the sake of the Lord. In the matter of origin, if a work is not from the Lord, the foundation of that particular task is faulty, and anything built on it will be faulty as well, regardless of outward appearances.

But many works have started with God and still ended in failure. That is because man begins to add his own ideas to the project. Since Christ must be "all-in-all," He must be the process as well as the origin. Whatever is done to carry out the plan of the work must be inspired by Christ and empowered by the Holy Spirit. If it is not, again, in spite of what might appear to be successful, the work passes from the realm of the spiritual to the carnal.

Jesus says it quite well in John 3:6, in which He points out that only Spirit can give birth to Spirit, and that flesh always gives birth to flesh. There can be no crossing over; each can only reproduce after its own kind. So once man adulterates God's idea with himself, the mixture becomes carnal, and therefore the result can only be carnal. From start to finish, any work done in the Name of the Lord must be *His work if it is to be rewarded; only these works are built of gold, silver, or precious stones and can stand the test of fire.*

Then of course, there is the matter of the success of the work: all the glory must go to the Lord. Pride must never enter the picture. So many men of God have been ensnared here! The Lord has initiated a work in them, they have carried it out by the empowerment of the Holy Spirit, and a marvelous thing has been produced by their faithfulness.

At first, the workers may have given all the glory to God, knowing that they alone could never have brought about such a glorious result. But then, little by little, pride begins to find a place in their hearts; they begin to think more highly of themselves than they ought. Surely, they reason, I must be special for God to do such a miracle through *me*. Soon a true work of God degenerates into a carnally-controlled enterprise of man, and the glory departs (whether anyone notices or not!).

Once the revelation of the mystery of the ages (Christ in you, the hope of glory) is fully discerned, and knowing this is the key to the eternal purpose of God (Christ being all-in-all), a measuring stick for all things spiritual is given. For this revelation and knowledge is the foundation of the "house" that we are; and not the foundation only, but every part of the house must be all Christ as well: the framing, the living stones, the covering (roof), all the interior, including the water, wiring, and plumbing. Nothing is to be a mixture of God and man. Christ must be all-in-all in the construction as well as the "running" of the house.

Of course, the family, the church, and the nation are composed of individual lives that are part of a bigger whole. If the individual has made Christ all-in-all in his life, that is the first step toward the healing of the family, church, and nation. It is also the first step toward the coming of the Kingdom! For the Lord is looking for such as these to rule and reign with Him. *They* are the spotless Bride, without blemish or wrinkles of any kind that the Spirit is preparing for the Son!

The foundation of any work in the Name of the Lord must be Christ alone. The same is true of the foundation of one's life; if the foundation is not Christ, nothing built will stand. But the materials of construction, the process of building and the results must be His as well. Anything less, any mixture of carnality with the spiritual, will be consumed at the judgment seat of Christ.

THREE CRUCIAL FACTS

For this is My blood of the new covenant, which is shed for many for the remission of sins."

Matthew 26:28

Blessed be the God and father of our Lord Jesus Christ, who has blessed us with every spiritual blessing in the Heavenly places in Christ, just as He chose us in Him before the foundation of the world, that we should be holy and without blame before Him in love.

Ephesians 1:3, 4

…knowing this, that our old man was crucified with Christ, that the body of sin might be done away with, that we should no longer be slaves of sin.

Romans 6:6

But God, who is rich in mercy, because of His great love with which He loved us, even when we were dead in trespasses, made us alive together with Christ (by grace you have been saved), and raised us up together in the Heavenly places in Christ Jesus, that in the ages to come He might show the exceeding riches of His grace in His kindness toward us in Christ Jesus.

Ephesians 2:4–7

> ...the mystery which has been hidden from ages and generations, but now has been revealed to His saints. To them God willed to make known what are the riches of the glory of this mystery among the Gentiles: which is Christ in you, the hope of glory.
>
> Colossians 1:26, 27

We have seen thus far that the eternal purpose of God is that His Son, the Lord Jesus Christ, be the sum of all things, all-in-all, being given the pre-eminence in all things (Col. 1:18). And moreover that Christ Himself is the plan of the Father to bring about that purpose: His perfect Life and the shedding of His precious Blood for our sins; our crucifixion, resurrection and ascension with Him; and His indwelling of us, His very Life becoming our life.

The Blood for us, being "in Him," and He being "in us": these are the provisions within the plan which will bring about all things being filled with nothing but the Life and glory of Christ. Three crucial facts to spiritually grasp and live if we are to overcome and reign with Christ in the coming Millennial Kingdom: we must overcome the penalty of sin, the power of sin, and the Law. Let us explore these glorious facts, one at a time, to show how victory is sure if we carefully take by faith and apply the perfect provisions the Lord God has placed at our disposal.

Jesus came as a man, born of a woman and under the Law, becoming what the Word calls the "second man and last Adam." What the first man, Adam, failed to accomplish, Jesus came to rectify. Three things were to be achieved: the redemption of fallen man from sin and death, the defeat of Satan and the fallen angels, and the regaining of the dominion given to man at his creation in Eden. These three accomplished and the way would be opened for the eternal purpose to be achieved.

As a man, Jesus had to first of all live a perfect life, without sin and relying totally on the Father, doing and saying only what the Father gave Him; never initiating *anything* on His own. As man, Jesus totally succeeded in all these areas. We know that by the Father's Word from Heaven that He was well-pleased in all of His beloved Son's thoughts, words, and actions. Further proof was given by Christ's resurrection from the dead and ascension into Heaven, where He is seated at His Father's right hand.

On the cross, Jesus also became the representative man, dying and becoming the perfect sacrifice for the sins of all men. He poured out His Blood and died as the penalty for sin, once and for all. All who believe in Him as Savior receive the remission of their sins and will not face the penalty for their transgressions; Jesus has already paid the price for them. When the Father looks upon any born-again believer, He sees the righteousness of His Son.

Hallelujah, what a Savior!

Jesus was raised from the dead on the third day and later, after appearing to His disciples and others many times, He was received into Heaven by the Father, signifying the defeat of Satan and the law of sin and death. At His coronation in the Heavenlies, Christ received the Holy Spirit in a new way: that He might pour it out on all those who would believe in Him unto new birth, and also for empowerment for the overcoming Life to which He would call them.

His call, of course, is to follow Him, overcoming the power of sin, Satan, and self, by making Him all-in-all, even as He had made the Father during His earthly sojourn. In other words, to utilize the anointing and in-filling of the Holy Spirit to have dominion over all things, including the deceptions and temptations of the enemy, thereby achieving the eternal purpose of God.

In becoming the Head, Christ has already accomplished His purpose. He is now waiting for a Body that will do likewise, a Bride without flaws of any kind. Removing those spots, blemishes and wrinkles is the work of the Holy Spirit.

But just how are we to do it, to go from a newborn babe in Christ to a fully mature overcomer? What provisions has the Father given to us, to take by faith and put into action, to achieve such a goal? It is critical that we understand and implement these provisions, for the very coming of the Kingdom, I believe, depends upon it.

The penalty for sin was paid for by Christ; it costs us nothing but repentance and belief, for we are "saved by grace through faith" (Ephesians 2:8). But how are we to overcome the power of sin? Certainly not by simply willing to do so and trying hard. There is in us what the Word calls the "old man," that fallen part of our nature inherited from Adam, that part that was born in sin and that loves to sin. What about him? For the power of sin continues to have its draw, even after rebirth.

Most believers, not knowing any better, set out to reform the old man, to make a better fellow of him (surely with the right training he can be brought under control). After many attempts and ensuing failures (sometimes lasting for years!) all of those who have followed this path come to conclude it is impossible. This is the moment the Holy Spirit has been waiting for, to show the aspiring disciple the true path to victory.

Romans 6:6 asserts quite firmly the fate of the old man: he was/is good for nothing but death! He is beyond repair; no amount of reform and patching up will ever make him acceptable to a holy God. He must die; and his death is exactly what the Father arranged. When Jesus was crucified, so was the old man. On first reading this fact, our mind, so confined to time and space, doesn't see how such a thing is possible. *How was I crucified with Christ two thousand years before I was born?* our reasoning objects. And certainly, "outside" God such a thing is inconceivable.

But of course, God is beyond the limitations of time and space, so human restrictions do not apply to Him. In Ephesians 1:3 and 4, we are told that those who belong to the Lord were chosen and placed "in Him" before the foundation of the world. Since those same ones can never be taken "out of Him," everywhere Christ has been, spiritually speaking, they have been. So when He was crucified, the fallen part of His own were crucified as well. This is an absolute spiritual fact and as such must be accepted by faith for it to become a living reality.

If we were crucified with Christ and are still in Him, then we were also raised when He was resurrected and ascended into Heavenly places at His ascension! Our crucifixion took care of the old man once and for all, and the new man, who arose with Christ, now sits in Heavenly places with Christ Jesus; all of this because we who are His have been "in Christ" from before the foundation of the world. In fact, there is nothing of spiritual value "outside" Christ; all the spiritual blessings we will ever enjoy are because we are in Him.

The shed Blood has secured our forgiveness and reconciliation with God; our old man has been disposed of by being crucified with Christ, and our new man has been raised and been made to sit in Heavenly places with Christ Jesus: all of this because the Father chose us before the foundation of the world and placed us in His Son!

What a plan! What a God we love and serve!

But there is yet more! The Father did not stop *there:* He also made a way for the very Life of His Son to come and live within us. This is what Colossians 1:26 calls the mystery of the ages, "Christ in you, the hope of glory." Without this provision, our new man could never achieve the eternal purpose of God. The key is "exchanged lives," the new man willingly giving up his own life in exchange for the Life of Christ; yielding to His Life, releasing Him to live His Life through us; this is the only way to complete victory.

God sees all of those who are His "finished" completely, what He created and ordained them to be. This is our position in Christ, but for it to become our actual experience as well, Christ in us must be "lived out." And hallelujah! The Father who called us to such a high calling has made a way for us to get there, now, in this life! Let us proceed and see how that works.

POSITION TO EXPERIENCE

> And we know that all things work together for good to those who love God, to those who are called according to His purpose. For whom He foreknew, He also predestined to be conformed to the image of His Son, that He might be the firstborn among many brethren. Moreover whom He predestined, these He also called; whom He called, these He also justified; and whom He justified, these He also glorified.
>
> Romans 8:28–30

The translation of our position in Christ to our experience is the work of the Holy Spirit. This process begins at the moment of our new birth. Through progressive revelation, the arrangement of circumstances, and even chastening when it is needed, the Spirit leads us to the end of ourselves, and from there, ever increasingly to Christ.

Of course this path is made more difficult by the attacks, deceptions, and constant interference of Satan and his hosts of demons and fallen angels. The last thing our enemy ever wants to happen is *maturity in Christ*. For when enough brothers and sisters in the Lord reach that point, our foe is finished. Tares, lookalikes, were planted amidst the wheat long ago, corrupting from within and building without, all in an effort to weaken the Body and prolong the devil's position as the ruler of this world.

But the next "fullness of time" is fast approaching, *the coming of the Kingdom*. More and more of the work of our enemy is being exposed and undone. To all those who have ears to hear and hearts to obey, wisdom and revelation are being poured out in ever-increasing waves. The keys to the Kingdom are being revealed, the willing hearts are emerging; all those who truly hunger and thirst after righteousness are being filled, putting His Kingdom and His righteousness *first*.

What are the provisions in Christ and He in us that will truly set us free to become who the Lord created us to be? There are many, but they all involve yielding to Christ that *He* might become all-in-all in every moment of our lives. After I had been teaching on the eternal purpose for some time, the Holy Spirit allowed me to go through an experience that demonstrated *in action* the very things He had previously taught me.

I am sure that I mentioned this before, but it is a lesson well worth repeating. For no apparent reason, all sorts of lustful thoughts began to invade my mind. I tried to ignore them, then tried to will them away, all to no avail. Of course, the enemy showed up and showered guilt and condemnation upon me (Why are you thinking such thoughts? I thought your old man was dead. Seems to me he's not... don't you see, this stuff you're teaching is just pie in the sky, and besides, with thoughts like that, *you* shouldn't be teaching such things at all. You're no good, etc.).

This went on for days. I really began suffering, with even doubt and the edge of depression creeping in. Then the Holy Spirit stepped in, and "said" something like this: "Don't you see what is happening here, son? Those thoughts are not your thoughts, the devil is impressing them upon you, hoping you would take them as your own. Of course your old nature is dead. He is attempting to use old man temptations to invade your new nature. And I am allowing it all to happen, to give you the opportunity to practice what you have been teaching."

As I waited upon Him for further instructions, He led me to 2 Corinthians 10, verses 3 to 5. As I read them, I sensed His prompting for me to decide what was the key word in that passage; I quote it here for your benefit: "For though we walk in the flesh, we do not war according to the flesh. For the weapons of our warfare are not carnal but mighty in God for pulling down strongholds, casting down vain imaginations and every high thing that exalts itself against the knowledge of God, bringing every thought into captivity to the obedience of Christ."

This is certainly a much-quoted portion of Scripture with which I was quite familiar. In prayer and spiritual warfare waged by believers, it is often pulled out as a weapon against the enemy, claiming our authority to pull down and cast out all that opposes God. But this was not what the Spirit was trying to reveal to me that day. Instead, He pointed out the next to last word, "of."

"Whose obedience are you to use, son?" He asked.

Christ's, of course! I realized immediately. There is no real authority except His. If He is all-in-all, and lives in me, that includes His perfect obedience. I must yield to that.

My next thought was this: *but how do I take those thoughts captive?* The answer was really quite simple: "You don't want them, do you?" The Spirit asked. *Of course not,* I thought. Then just take them, give them to the Lord, and ask for His obedience to come forth, the Spirit prompted.

I obeyed, and the thoughts disappeared! They left as though they had never been there. I was amazed at how simple the whole thing was: no struggles, no strain, just letting His Life in this particular situation be released. And I have continued to use this practical weapon anytime anything has tried to "exalt itself against the knowledge of God," and it has worked time and again. It is Life of Christ within that must be "lived out" if victory is to come!

And I know the answer will be the same no matter the situation and need: if it is forgiveness I cannot muster on my own, He will give me His; if the need is for mercy, His, not mine. Patience? His! Peace? His! (This same revelation and its application has set one person I counseled free from a long-standing addiction to alcohol, with no need to go to a rehabilitation center. Properly discerned and applied, I am convinced it will do the same for anyone, no matter the problem. The Life of Christ unleashed can defeat any and all the bondages the enemy has established in our lives!)

I realized that this is the "way of escape" to be taken anytime trials or temptations befall us. Christ is the way of escape. He is the door to victory in all such situations. Hallelujah! He truly is everything, all-in-all, the sum of all things! I had known this before, *in theory* so to speak, but now I knew in reality, by experiencing it!

The Holy Spirit also instructed me to fill the void left by the exit of those impure thoughts with more of Him, to praise Him for the victory, giving Him all the glory; to fill myself with the things of Paul's exhortation in Philippians 4:8: "Finally, brethren, whatever things are true, whatever things are noble, whatever things are just, whatever things are pure, whatever things are lovely, whatever things are of good report, if there is any virtue, and if there is anything praiseworthy—meditate on these things."

All of these "things" are Christ, of course, different aspects of His perfection and fullness; so when I thought on them, I remembered that they are in fact Him. He whose very Life is within me, and available to become my own if I will simply be willing to "die daily" (1 Corinthians 15:31). The new man that I am in Christ must come into an ever-increasing dimension of yielding to Him; and this willing surrender must be during "good times" and everyday living, as well as during times of crisis.

I repeat, not only during times of crisis, but during the "good times" as well!

What a place of rest! And a place of peace, being "anxious for nothing" (Phil. 4:6). Knowing whose hands I am in, being re-molded into His image and likeness, becoming exactly who He ordained and created me to be; living in such a way that will "hasten the coming of the day of the Lord" (2 Peter 3:12).

LOVE AND OBEDIENCE

For though we walk in the flesh, we do not war according to the flesh. For the weapons of our warfare are not carnal but mighty in God for pulling down strongholds, casting down arguments and every high thing that exalts itself against the knowledge of God, bringing every thought into captivity to the obedience of Christ.

2 Corinthians 10:3–5

He who has my commandments and keeps them, it is he who loves Me. And he who loves Me will be loved by My Father, and I will love him and manifest Myself to him.

John 14:21

Jesus answered and said, 'If anyone loves Me, he will keep My word; and My Father will love him, and We will come to him and make our home with him.'

John 14:23

If you abide in Me, and My words abide in you, you will ask what you desire, and it shall be done for you.

John 15:7

There exists a strong connection between our love for God and our obedience to Him. Under the Law, obedience came mainly from a sense of duty and even fear of the wrath of God for disobedience. It was not until Jesus came that obedience issued from love. He so loved the Father and was so fully submitted to Him that obeying all the Father desired was as natural for Christ as sinning is for the sinner.

In John 14 and 15, Jesus taught that love and obedience are inextricably bound; that if we truly love Him, we will keep His commandments. And that through our obedience more of His love would be released within us. With more love released, obedience would be its natural outworking, which in turn would yield more love; and so the joyous cycle would go.

Of course, the moment the Holy Spirit fills us with the Life of Christ, all the Lord's love fills us as well; more is not added later. But until self is surrendered, little by little, the fullness of that love remains latent within us. With each submission of our soul life unto the Lord in obedience, more love is released to us, which causes our love for the Lord to increase, and our desire to obey Him to likewise increase.

When this process is completed, the exchange of our life for His will have taken place, God's eternal purpose achieved, and the Father and the Son will come to abide (make their home with us!), never to leave again.

But as we have seen before, even that obedience is Him, His obedience. Second Corinthians 10:3–5 states that it is to *His* obedience that we must take captive all opposing thoughts, temptations, imaginations, and self-exalting knowledge; that part of Himself within us, which loved and obeyed the Father even unto the death on the cross. There and there alone lies the victory! He must be all-in-all, even our obedience.

A reading of the great love chapter, 1 Corinthians 13, reveals a level of love beyond human ability, a love that can only be Christ Himself. And the fruit of the Spirit listed in Galatians 5:22–23 are all qualities of that love. His love will always express itself through joy, peace, longsuffering, kindness, goodness, faithfulness, gentleness, and self-control. And these are the very fruits that will be produced in us once His Life becomes our Life. Outside Christ Himself, such things simply do not exist.

While we were yet sinners outside Christ, we did not have to *try* to sin, did we? No, that which was in us just naturally came out. To put it another way, *life just lives!* The same holds true for the Life of Christ within us: it simply lives out what it is! We do not have to pursue the fruits of the Spirit; in fact, such a pursuit will always prove futile, and can only produce man-made look-alikes. The real things will always elude such attempts.

Here it might serve our purpose to differentiate the gifts of the Spirit from the Spirit's fruit: Gifts are just what they say—they are *gifts!* They come to each believer free of charge, gifts from the risen Savior via the Holy Spirit to equip us for certain aspects of the ministry of the Word, and to serve as signs of validation for the Diety of Christ.

Fruit, on the other hand, is not freely given; it is quite costly, for it calls for the surrender of self to the Holy Spirit. More surrender, more fruit, for with obedience comes more love released, which in turn yields more obedience. Eventually, we are so constrained by the love of Christ that obedience comes "naturally," the living out of the Life within us.

Such fruit is certainly painful to the flesh, for it is only produced by our daily dying to our own ideas, feelings, and decisions. But once we begin to understand what the Lord is doing through such trials, His Life for ours, we not only come to accept them but to rejoice when these hard times come. For this is the way we become partakers of His very nature!

FIRST LOVE

> Nevertheless I have *this* against you, that you have left your first love. Remember therefore from where you have fallen; repent and do the first works, or else I will come to you quickly and remove your lampstand from it place—unless you repent.
>
> Revelation 2:4–5

After commending the church at Ephesus for their works, labor, and patience, for their discernment concerning false brethren, the Lord found a single fault; but one so serious that the church's very existence depended upon its correction: leaving their first love for Him. What a serious point to consider!

The believers there were commanded to repent of this great sin and to return to their first works. First love, of course, is meant to develop into mature love, following the cycle of love and obedience previously discussed. But at Ephesus, first love had been "left" (but not lost, thank God!), obedience perhaps diminishing to a sense of duty and the works done in that same spirit as well. Such works rapidly become carnal, no longer of any spiritual value.

With first love left behind, it was inevitable that true obedience would suffer as well. For it is in genuine love that obedience manifests itself. Less love, less obedience; less obedience, less love, a process that in time provides the enemy an inroad for sin. False teaching finds its way in by this means as well. Sound teaching is no longer accepted, compromise and cheap grace set in, and soon the height from which one has fallen is no longer remembered. Some other gospel becomes a way of life!

As we study church history, we come to see that is exactly what has happened! After suffering at Smyrna, false teaching crept in at Pergamos, and by the time we reach Thyratira, the whole system had become corrupt, controlled by a false prophetess named Jezebel. Then after some sort of renewal, the church at Sardis returned to at least certain foundational truths, and as a result had a reputation for being alive. But the Lord still judged the believers at Sardis as falling short, and commanded them to "strengthen" the things that remained.

The church at Philadelphia is a very interesting case. They either came out of the renewal at Sardis by going beyond the shortcomings there; or they represent the remnant of believers who never strayed from the true gospel of the Kingdom. In either case, they are a picture of the true church. No criticism was given by the Lord at Philadelphia. Instead they were highly commended.

The believers at Philadelphia had only a "little strength," but had kept His Word (obedience), not denied His Name, and had kept the Word of *His* patience. From this foundation, they had done their works (of love) and had recognized and rejected false teaching. For this the Lord promised them that He would keep them *from* the "hour of trial which shall come upon the whole world, to test those who dwell on the earth" (Rev. 3:10).

By the time we reach the Lord's judgment of the church at Laodicea, we find that believers there had only a form of godliness, but no real substance. While thinking themselves "rich" (spiritually and materially), they were actually destitute: the Lord called them "wretched, miserable, poor, blind, and naked" (verse 3:17). The result of this condition was lukewarm-ness toward the things of God; and without deep repentance, the Lord declared He would vomit them out of His mouth!

Many believe Laodicea is a picture of much of the church today, especially in places like America, where wealth and materialism have run rampant. Lukewarm love can never produce true obedience, and lukewarm obedience can never release more genuine love. We must repent! Repent and cry out to the Lord for a return to our first love, or to whatever stage our love began to cool off. We must see that only Christ coming forth in our lives can ever produce fruit that lasts, the fruit of His love!

KINGDOM FRUIT

> But the fruit of the Spirit is love, joy, peace, long-suffering, kindness, goodness, faithfulness, gentleness, self-control. Against such there is no law. And those who are Christ's have crucified the flesh with its passions and desires. If we live in the Spirit, let us also walk in the Spirit.
>
> Galatians 5:22–25

> For the Kingdom of God is not in word but in power.
>
> 1 Corinthians 4:20

> But if I cast out demons by the Spirit of God, surely the Kingdom of God has come upon you.
>
> Matthew 12:28

> Most assuredly, I say to you, he who believes in Me, the works that I do he will do also; and greater works than these he will do, because I go to My Father.
>
> John 14:12

It is interesting that the grammar in Galatians 5:22 and 23 indicates that all the nine "fruits" of the Spirit are actually only one; fruit "is," not fruits "are." That is because all these various things are in fact Christ; they do not exist outside Him; He is all these and everything else spiritual as well! So we must not go after *them*, but only Him.

Living the true Kingdom Life *has* to yield "fruit that lasts." Perhaps all of the fullness of that Life will not manifest until Christ returns, but we are to experience now at least a "foretaste of the power of the age to come" (Hebrews 6:5). After Jesus was baptized by both John the Baptist and the Holy Spirit (and the Father proclaimed His affirmation from Heaven), and He then defeated the enemy in His test in the wilderness, great power came upon the Lord. Everywhere He went people were healed and set free: infirmities, blindness, deafness, demon possession, all began to go; even the dead were raised back to life!

The early church also began to experience miracles of the same kind. Peter, Paul, John, all of them walked in power that confirmed the Word of the Kingdom they were announcing. The same should hold true today. Indeed, Jesus declared in John 14:12 that those who believe in Him would do those same works, and even greater works than He performed. So long as His own people (the Jews) and most of the rest of the world reject Him, those works may not become normative, but they should not be completely missing, or at best, extremely rare.

Jesus was the first man who entered the Kingdom (by making the Father all-in-all), but He is to be only the firstborn among *many* brethren. It is time for the sons of God to be revealed and begin to manifest themselves; nature itself is crying out for it! The full truth of the gospel, which the enemy has been so adept at hiding and thwarting, is now coming to light.

The gifts of the Holy Spirit are just that, gifts, free and without cost to their recipients. The anointing the Lord is now preparing to pour out is much greater than those, for the cost of what is coming is *everything*, even our own lives. Just how the anointing will manifest, I do not know; as in all things, I leave that up to the Lord. But I find myself longing and praying for it more and more; not to bring glory to myself or to any man, but to the Lord alone.

Paul said in 1 Corinthians 4:20 that the Kingdom is about more than just talk. It is also accompanied by the power of the Holy Spirit. And Jesus Himself said that if He casts out demons by the Spirit of God, know this: the Kingdom has come upon you! (Matt. 12:28). We should experience this same "coming" of the Kingdom, working all the works that Jesus worked (and more, whatever that could be!).

It is our heritage in the Lord, the return of the dominion over all things that Jesus regained on our behalf. It is ours now, the Body of Christ in perfect submission to the Head and to one another, doing all the will of the Father, making Him the God of Heaven *and* earth once again. This is the way the Kingdom will be ushered in, by the willing hearts in this, "the day of His battle..." (Psalm 110:3).

THE FULLNESS OF TIME

> But when the fullness of time had come, God sent forth His Son, born of a woman, born under the law, to redeem those who were under the law, that we might receive the adoption as sons.
>
> Galatians 4:4, 5

> Let not your heart be troubled, you believe in God, believe also in Me. In My Father's house are many mansions; if it were not so, I would have told you. I go to prepare a place for you. And if I go and prepare a place for you, I will come again and receive you to Myself; that where I am, there you may be also.
>
> John 14:1–3

> For the earnest expectation of the creation eagerly waits for the revealing of the sons of God.... Not only that, but we also who have the first fruits of the Spirit, even we ourselves groan within ourselves, eagerly waiting for the adoption, the redemption of our body.
>
> Romans 8:19, 23

The "fullness of time" is such a pregnant phrase! We know that eventually time shall be no more; and that time only came into existence because of sin (birth, life, and death required it). Even during the Millennium, the clock will be ticking, marking off the seconds, minutes, hours, days, months, and years until the thousand years will have ended.

But the history of man has been measured by time, different eras, different ways in which God has dealt with His fallen creation, bringing it ever so gradually to the fulfillment of His eternal purpose. Once that is achieved, time will have outlived its usefulness and will disappear into eternity.

Time has reached its fullness several times in the past. The Age of Innocence in the Garden began at creation and extended until the fall of man: the fullness of that time period had been reached, thus the ending of one era and the beginning of a new one. The new dispensation became the Age of Conscience, for with his fall into sin, man became conscious of right and wrong.

Time again reached its fullness when evil abounded to the extent that the judgment of God became necessary: with the exceptions of Noah and his family (and the animals Noah was commanded to save), the Great Flood destroyed all life upon the earth.

After the flood, the descendants of Shem, Ham, and Japheth established what might be called the Age of Human Government; which was short-lived (approximately four hundred years), from the Flood to the building of the Tower of Babel. Due to the confusion of languages at Babel, however, even the sons of Ham were dispersed throughout the globe (even as God had commanded), and men formed their own type of government wherever they settled.

The next era of time began with the call of Abraham, the Lord God's calling of a particular people unto Himself. We might call this period of time the Age of Promise; for with the call of Abraham came many promises by God, all of which would eventually lead to the coming of the promised seed of the woman, who would crush the head of the great serpent (Satan).

The Age of Promise reached its fullness with the coming of the Law on Mount Sinai. God dealt with His chosen people through the Law for almost fifteen hundred years, from the days of Moses until the coming of Christ; teaching them that there is no way back to Him by the works done in their own power. In fact, the Age of the Law did not reach its fullness until the death, resurrection, and ascension of the Lord. With the outpouring of the Holy Spirit on the day of Pentecost, the Age of the Law gave way to the Age of Grace.

The Age of Grace has been heading toward the next great dispensation, the Age of the Kingdom, for over two thousand years. The Holy Spirit has been gathering those who belong to the Lord, forming them into a Body (and from the Body a Bride) for Christ, perfecting them by the Life of Christ, removing all obstacles that stand in the way of the eternal purpose of the Father.

There have been times in which I have felt very discouraged; so few seem to be responding to the gospel of the Kingdom. The masses (and the church) seem satisfied with the status quo, things going on as they always have. But then the Spirit reminded me that there have been over fifty generations since the coming of Christ; and that every generation has had its faithful remnant, slowly adding to the number of overcomers. And that for critical mass to be reached, only the smallest part has to be added from this generation for a chain reaction to take place, ushering in the Kingdom!

Yes, Lord, time is again approaching its fullness; the Age of the Kingdom is just over the horizon. The deceptions of the enemy are being uncovered, the willing hearts are beginning to appear, all prophecy is reaching its fulfillment, and the Bride is almost ready! The cry is about to go forth that the Bridegroom is coming. Get ready, people; wake up, He's coming!

SUMMING UP

I am encouraged that others are rediscovering the gospel of the Kingdom and its importance in the total scheme of things. God is no respecter of persons, so I knew He had to be giving others in the Body revelations similar to my own. As to the eternal purpose of God, I have come across at least two other ideas concerning this all-important matter.

One brother has rightly claimed that the Father's eternal purpose is love; that since God *is* love, no purpose could be higher. I agree with that, but I also assert that love with no trace of hatred or fear can only come about when Christ becomes all-in-all; until then, there will always be a place, no matter how small, for something else to creep in.

Another brother has correctly proclaimed that God's eternal purpose is to lead many sons to glory. While I agree that many sons (and daughters) will indeed be led to glory, I must again insist that such a glorious event cannot take place until Christ becomes the sum of all things; for it is only by this very process that *any* son can ever be led to glory. There is no other way to glory for anyone.

Once clearly seen, the way from sin and the world to the Kingdom is simple and direct. What has made it so difficult are the tenacity of self and the deceptions of the enemy. But little by little for the persevering believer, a way is being made by God where there seemed to be no way. Pray for more and more wandering pilgrims to find their way back to that simple path, and for new believers to see it from the very beginning of their walk. Even so, come quickly, Lord Jesus!

AFTERWORD

A young man at the Christian rehabilitation center where I teach, after hearing a series on the eternal purpose of God, asked, "Are you *there*, brother Rod?"

I thought it a great question and immediately answered, "No, not yet. But I know where *there* is now. And just as importantly, I know where there is *not*."

Then the Lord gave me the words of Paul in Philippians 3:13–14:

> Brethren, I do not count myself to have apprehended; but one thing I do, forgetting those things which are behind and reaching forward to those things which are ahead, I press toward the goal for the prize of the upward call of God in Christ Jesus.

We must press on toward our *full* inheritance in Christ, forgetting all the failures of the past and looking toward the coming Kingdom. Paul described in Galatians 2:20 what had become living reality for him, and it must become our own experience as well:

> I have been crucified with Christ; it is no longer I who live, but Christ lives in me; and the *life* which I now live in the flesh I live by faith in the Son of God, who loved me and gave Himself for me.

Kingdom Perspective

Lord, grant us Kingdom perspective,
This view we must seek first...
Allow Your Life to fully live,
O satisfy this thirst!

Your true church You said You would build,
Our focus on the Rock;
We simply do what You have willed,
And Kingdom will unlock...

Let this be our continual desire and fervent prayer until we see Him face-to-face.

Amen

OTHER WORKS BY ROD CONNELL

Silly Snake Rhymes ... And the Real Stuff

> A perfect blend of fun and fact,
> Designed to tickle and attract!
> Mankind's serpent fascination
> In cartoon and education...
> To see how the silliness ends,
> Come, let's join our wriggling friends!

"*Silly Snake Rhymes* is slithery fun for children and the adults who read these funny poems aloud to them. Whether you love snakes already or aren't quite sure, you will love them by the time you finish this book of funny, light verse and humorous illustrations. By the time readers have warmed up to the snakes, the 'real stuff' offers scientific information about each species cited in the poems."

—Linda Chapman,
VP of Academic Affairs,
Lewis and Clark Community College

"*Silly Snake Rhymes* is a poetry book with witty wordplay and clever drawings. From Wanda, the anaconda who loves riding a Honda, to Elvis, the king cobra with a pierced fang, every page is a delight. The book was created as a collaboration between a grandfather and his grandson, and its appeal, quite literally, will span the generations."

—Terri R. Hilgendorf,
English & Literature Coordinator,
Lewis and Clark Community College

Available for $10.99 from author at hidvalley@frontiernet.net or Amazon.com and tatepublishing.com

Songs of a Son

Songs of a Son is an inspiring collection of spiritual poetry.

More information is available at the author's website, www.eternalppp.com.